MONEY MASTER OF THE WORLD

WILLARD CANTELON

Logos International
Plainfield, New Jersey

Grateful acknowledgment is given to *Newsweek* magazine for permission to reprint the table on page 29 herein which is copyright 1976 by Newsweek Inc.

To Verna

CONTENTS

FOREWORD

Many years ago, as a young banker, I met Willard Cantelon in person, when he spoke in our city. After that first meeting, our paths took each of us in opposite directions. I remained with the bank in our state, while Cantelon chose to study the part played by finance in the trend toward one world government.

When our paths crossed once again after many years, many changes had taken place in our world. I viewed the world as an American banker who had spent forty-three years with the Federal Reserve Bank, while Cantelon had devoted much of his life to the study of international finance at home and abroad.

Willard Cantelon, in my opinion, possesses two unusual qualities. As a conservative, he does not resent "one worlders" and listens with an open mind to the views of others. His book, I am sure, will prove most fascinating to ordinary laymen, as well as to veteran bankers such as me.

Edward P. Farley

Chapter 1
Why Did He Die?

Under a warmer than usual California sun, I turned my car into Glendale Avenue and drove in the direction of Algemac's Restaurant. The clock in the car told me that I was early for my appointment with Joe Baumgartner, so I slackened my pace to enjoy the beauties of this little city that we presently called home.

A gentle breeze from the Pacific caused the palms to toss their fronds playfully against a cloudless sky. The fruitstands and florist shops along the avenue provided enough color and flavor to suggest that this might well be Eden restored, and the men walking lazily in the sunshine were masters of their world.

In one instant, however, the entire scene changed. Through the open gates of Forest Lawn I glimpsed not only the fountain weaving its white pattern against the green of the lawns and trees, I also saw the funeral chapel on the top of the hill. The sight of this chapel flooded my memory with a scene of sorrow from the previous week. By the casket containing the body of a loved one, mourners with eyes red

1

from weeping had turned to me sadly and asked, "Why did he have to die when he was so young?"

Evidence of Fear

Arriving early at the restaurant, I seated myself at a corner table from which I could watch for the arrival of my friend. When I saw Joe in the doorway, I smiled and thought, "How could I miss him? Who today walks or drives as fast as he?"

"Well, friend," said Joe, after his usual handshake and greeting. "What's on your mind?"

"A funeral," I replied.

His brows raised quizzically, and Joe looked at me as if to say that he was not sure if I were serious or not.

I continued, "I realize we didn't meet today to talk about the dead, but when you asked what was on my mind, I had to be honest. I was at Cliff's funeral last week; his family was heartbroken; they asked me, 'Why did he have to die?' "

"Cancer, wasn't it?" asked Joe.

"True," I answered slowly. "But why does cancer claim so many victims today? These days are not like the dark ages, when the Black Plague moved across nations unchallenged and unchecked. This is the day of miracle drugs and unparalleled achievements of the medical world. But in spite of all our wisdom and wonder drugs, some medical men are suggesting that cancer may soon be striking one out of four people. And," I added, "many of these young people."

"With all the millions spent on research, I wonder how near we may be to finding a cure for cancer?" asked Joe, with his eyes fixed on the table.

"That is hard to say, but one thing does seem certain. There is more agreement on the 'cause' of cancer than there is on the cure. Right here on the newsstand last week, I picked up a paper with a headline that said **90% of Sickness Related to Fears for the Financial Future.**"

2

"Wouldn't you consider that an overstatement?"

"Possibly, but there is undoubtedly much truth in it. As far back as 1912, Dr. Alexis Carrell, who won the Nobel Prize, declared that most sickness was related to fear. And when one considers that man's money buys his food, clothing, pleasures, and future security, he naturally is concerned about its value for the future."

The Anxiety of the Aged

"Older people who, in their early lives, earned dollars which they hoped would be adequate to sustain them in old age, have seen the value of their money erode with inflation."

"True," replied Joe. "I suppose some old folks feel that the dollars of their youthful years are worth only dimes today."

"The future for Social Security is not too comforting to think about either," I added. "When I was in Dallas a month or two ago, it seemed that the front pages of the press for an entire week carried articles suggesting that Social Security might not survive. The Dallas papers, of course, were no exceptions; even in *Nation's Business*, Robert Gray candidly asks, **Will the Social Security Bubble Burst?** (November 1974).

"When a city like New York suddenly finds its coffers empty, how can it meet its welfare payments? The cost must be staggering. Eight percent of the city's seven million drew some form of welfare, and a mother with two children could receive as much as $200 a month. Last year alone, the nation paid over $24 billion in welfare to three and a half million families."

"Regarding New York City," continued Joe, "they've had to take some rather drastic steps, haven't they?"

"How would you like to hear tomorrow that Los Angeles, for lack of funds to pay salaries, was laying off a thousand policemen?"

"Not very well, with over 1600 murders registered here last year. Crime is more a part of life than ever," said Joe.

"How well I know."

Joe turned abruptly, sensing in the tone of my voice more than a casual comment and asked, "When were you last in New York?"

"Last Thanksgiving. For twenty years, I have spoken at an annual convention there when I have been in the country. But I never experienced anything like what happened this time in those two previous decades."

"Why do you say that?"

Unwelcome Guests

"Because at 1:30 one afternoon two men using a passkey entered my room on the eighth floor of my hotel, and demanded my wallet."

"That must have been quite a sensation."

"Yes it was. One reads about such experiences happening every day, but you never dream it could happen to you personally."

"I would call you a fortunate victim," said Joe with a grin.

"And I would agree."

"After lunch I decided to do some recording in my room. I had brought with me from Los Angeles a Nagra IV recorder, which was worth close to $2,000. When I realized that I needed an extra take-up reel, I put my coat and hat on and ran across to Macy's to buy it. A few yards down the hall, I noticed a fellow dressed like a serviceman ask the maid on the floor if he could plug an extension cord into my room."

"Did you wonder why in your room?"

"Yes, but only for a moment. There had been a convention in the hotel and most of the people were checking out. I was one of the few remaining guests on the eighth floor.

"As you know, I have lived much of my life in hotels, and am accustomed to service personnel coming and going. I

4

dismissed the thought with a shrug of the shoulders and went on my way."

"Do you think the fellow was stalking the place to see what guests were still in the hotel with valuable belongings?"

"I think so, Joe, because several others were involved beside the man with the extension cord. He probably noted in my absence that I had an expensive recorder and other valuables in my room, and notified the younger men who were actually set for the break-in.

"After making my purchase in Macy's, I was back in the hotel within three quarters of an hour, probably earlier than they expected. On the eighth floor, I noticed two men walking down the corridor ahead of me."

"You were behind them so they did not see you?"

"Yes, I don't think they saw me enter my room."

"Maybe they didn't expect you to be in the room when they entered?"

"That could be, Joe. I had just hung up my coat when I heard a key turning in my lock."

"Didn't you have the safety lock on?"

"No, Joe, and that has been a failing of mine all my life. Verna has corrected me, especially in recent years for seldom using the second lock on the hotel door when I am in the room."

"I'll bet you will remember now."

"You can be sure I will."

"Do you know how these fellows got the key to your room?"

"Yes. I learned they forced the maid to surrender her key to them."

"Do you suppose she was involved?"

"Hard to say . . . it is possible."

Give Us Your Wallet or We'll Kill You

"When I heard the key turning the lock of my door, I

moved quickly to see who it was, but they rushed in with the announcement, 'This is a holdup, lie on the bed or we'll kill you.' "

"And did you?"

"No, I did not."

"So, what then?"

"Well, they kept repeating this over and over, and I continued to refuse."

"Did they have guns or knives?"

"I couldn't tell. You see the short passage to the door of my room was narrow and when they entered they pushed me back into the corner, and continued to hold me there."

"I bet it seemed like hours."

"They kept repeating, 'Give us your wallet or we'll kill you.' "

"Did you?"

"No, because in my wallet I had three one-hundred-dollar bills, credit cards, a check from a missions board, and identification papers. I could not see parting with them to these fellows."

Faith or Folly?

"Weren't you taking a foolhardy risk, Willard?"

"Joe," I replied slowly, "one cannot predict his actions, or, should I say, reactions, when such a thing strikes so unexpectedly. It is not something you meditate beforehand and say, 'Now, if such-and-such should happen, I would do this or that.' No, as I look back, I know there is only one reason I acted as I did. I had commenced the day with my usual prayer of thanks to God for His blessings and protection in the past, and also for the present. So, all of the time that these fellows were saying, 'Give us your wallet or we'll kill you,' something inwardly was saying, 'No they won't; just give them a little money and outtalk them.' And that is exactly what I did. While holding my wallet firmly in my hands, I removed some small bills and took off my wristwatch, which was one of the oldest and cheapest watches that I owned. I gave them this watch and the small bills, and said, 'This is absolutely all that I am giving you.' "

"And they left?"

"Right."

"Unbelievable. And they did not get your recorder?"

"No, thank God. I found myself unharmed, and still in possession of the recorder and wallet and most of its contents."

"Do you know how much you gave them?"

"No," I said with a laugh. I didn't bother to count it. But I customarily keep larger bills in the back section of my wallet, and the small bills in the front. I was happy to keep my large bills and my cards and papers. I didn't complain about losing the small change."

"Nor would I," said Joe thoughtfully. "What was your next move?"

One Out of Five Caught and Punished

"I immediately phoned to report the theft to the hotel desk and police."

"And were they caught?"

"Not while I was there. I heard the guards say it was one of the most brazen robberies they had experienced in that hotel. The hotel had been quite full, and the lower lobby was congested with people checking out, as well as a new crowd coming in. They got away. After all, I believe even the national rate today shows that only about twenty percent of such offenders are caught and punished.

Financial Problems

"With New York laying off police, I am sure the crime scene won't improve."

"No, Joe, it won't. When the city went into its crisis of 1975, they laid off 5000 police, and about 1800 firemen."

7

"Because they were not able to pay salaries?"

"Right. In May of 1975, Mayor Beame went to Washington to say the city needed another billion dollars in aid from the federal government before June. If I remember correctly, New York was already receiving about two and a third billion from Washington for various programs."

"And," added Joe, "I believe that Mr. Simon, secretary of the treasury, and President Ford, turned down that first appeal."

"Not surprising. After all, what happens when the federal government runs out of money, where does a city go then? In New York, nearly one out of eight in the city's 7.6 million receives welfare. The city, state, and federal aid for New York in a single year ran about $2.6 billion.

Food Stamps

"Look for example just at the food stamp program. It costs the government almost $6 billion a year. That is almost two thirds of the total budget for the Department of Agriculture. The secretary of the treasury in a speech in Bloomington, Indiana, said 'it was a program that was spinning out of control.' "

"I think it has become a racket with some also, hasn't it?"

"Yes," I replied. "According to Carl Williams, deputy U.S. commissioner of welfare, billions of dollars are being given away with virtually no control. Williams said for those who wanted to be crooked it is an easy matter to sell $100 worth of food stamps on the black market for $80. The buyer can sell them in turn to a grocer for $90, who can turn them to the government for $100.

Under the Lash of Federal Law

"Figures released by the Agriculture Department show that:

In 1970—6.5 million received food stamps;

In 1971—10.5 million received food stamps;

In 1975—19.2 million received food stamps.

No wonder Mr. Simon said it is spinning out of control. Some have suggested that the present rate of increase would indicate that soon 30 to 40 million would be receiving food stamps."

"And," added Joe, "many who don't deserve them."

"That is the big problem. The federal government continues to enact more laws in their futile effort to control abuses. It costs $5.00 for administration for every $1.00 food stamp given away.

"I believe it was Casper Weinberger, former secretary of health, education and welfare, who said, 'The entire human-resources field is under the lash of federal law' " (*Readers Digest*, page 94, November 1975).

"Let's get back to those fellows who robbed you, Willard. Were they young?"

"I'd judge they were in their twenties."

"Probably unemployed, frustrated and bitter," added Joe.

"And," I continued, "maybe too proud to ask for food stamps if hungry."

The Frustrations of Youth

"Today's youth have some very real problems, even those who are educated. Not too long ago, an issue of *Time* spread an article over several pages depicting the problems of educated young people. It cited the experiences of fellows like Mark Steinberg, 25, a Phi Beta Kappa graduate from U.C.L.A., with an M.A. in psychology from Berkeley, subsisting on food stamps and welfare in Venice, California. When asked how many responses he had had to the fifty resumes he sent out, he replied, 'One.' "

The National Board on Graduate Education estimated that through the end of the 1970's, as few as seven thousand Ph.D.'s a year, or a fifth of the thirty-five thousand or more produced, will find work closely related to their training (*Time*, March 29, 1976).

"Some of the pictures and articles in the news media are anything but inspiring to the young. One recent issue of a national magazine was filled with scenes of the Great Depression. It told of a quarter of the nation's laborers being unemployed; of young parents going home to their own parents with the grandchildren in tow, causing the old folks to mortgage their homes or farms to feed them, and finally to lose all that they had saved.

"Another article mentioned a college lad who hitchhiked thirty miles on Sundays to visit his brother, and get a square meal."

"I remember in our local paper," continued Joe, "a picture of thousands of men standing in line at Christmas time in Cleveland, waiting to get their pound of rice and a few oranges."

"The news media has a way of periodically reminding the young 'It could happen again.' "

The Fears of the Housewives

"How many times in supermarkets have you seen shoppers studying the code markings on the packages of food and asking, 'Is this preparation for rationing?' "

"Some people are old enough to remember the rationing of war days, when the little ration coupon took precedence over money as a medium of exchange. And, if a man were honest, he knew that the rich man received the same allotment of sugar, shoes, coffee, and gasoline, as the poorest man in town."

"Bad as it may have been in America," added Joe, "it was mild, compared to Europe."

"That's true, Joe. I recall the English telling me of their years of rationing, when at its worst, a man's weekly allowance included only one egg and two ounces of meat."

"They must have filled up on potatoes and biscuits," added Joe, as he looked at the plates of food that the waitress had brought for our lunch. "Things are certainly different today."

"And," I added, "serious-minded men know that changes can come suddenly. There are two kinds of crises; one is military, and one is monetary. Right now, the British are talking about rationing gasoline."

"And we almost had it rationed in 1973, didn't we? Were you in Europe or America then?"

"Both."

"What was the attitude of the Europeans that year?"

"I would say much the same as the attitude here, quite frustrated. When we were in Germany, Belgium and Holland, where heavy fines were imposed for driving cars on certain Sundays, people asked how this could be necessary, when oil tankers were at anchor in almost every seaport of northern Europe, unable to unload their cargo because every European storage tank on the continent was full."

"And speaking of rationing, not too much was said about the 4,800,000,000 gas ration coupons that were printed and never used. One reason possibly was because the designer had unknowingly made the coupons resemble a one dollar bill so closely that the coupon could be inserted in place of a dollar in a money changer, and release a dollar's worth of coins."

"Did they destroy the coupons?"

"No, I understand they are still in storage. After all, it cost the taxpayers $12.5 million to print them."

"Do you suppose they will eventually be used?"

"I doubt it. If and when rationing comes, we will undoubtedly see a single card used. Even last summer in Germany, when we stopped at the Holiday Inn in Munchingen, we were given a little brochure telling how the Holiday Inns of

11

the world could register their 300,000 reservations daily on their world-wide network, with *every* reservation being cleared in seconds in Memphis, Tennessee, using computers linked by satellite."

The Farmers' Fears

"With the way things have been going, lots of people have gotten in the mood to move to the country. They hope to find security by owning land. But the landowners who remember the 1930's are haunted by the recollection of one of Franklin Roosevelt's "Fireside Chats." In it the president announced that there would soon be a "Tough New Set of Rules." Few farmers who heard that announcement realized just how "tough" those rules would be."

"Under the New Deal, one could no longer decide personally what acreage he could plant. And even though the farm was his own, he was restricted as to what he could sow and reap. The prices of produce sank so low in those days that many farmers lost their land on tax foreclosures."

"Do you suppose this could happen again?"

"If a similar crisis should come, legislation is ready for enforcement. On June 21st, 1973, the Senate, by a vote of 64-21, passed the 'Land Use Policy and Planning Assistance Act.' On the surface, it appeared to be a bill that would help farmers in times of crisis, but on closer scrutiny men such as Senator Paul Fannin, who voted for its passage, became alarmed at the controls it could bring. He said: 'It would do great violence to American rights . . . and reduce landowners to landless serfs,' " (Publication: Committee to Restore the Constitution, January 15, 1974).

With computer control, some say this bill could govern the use of every foot of ground whether on ranches or farms, or in city gardens.

Bankrupt Businessmen

We pushed back our empty plates and noticed that the

noon crowd in the restaurant was leaving. Only a few tables remained filled.

But Joe, who was usually in a hurry, seemed inclined to sit and talk further.

"The general public has adjusted to the higher prices at the present," said Joe slowly, "and has almost forgotten that the energy shortage wiped out countless small independent dealers."

"Not only here, but in Europe too," I added. "Dr. Wilhelm Noelling, the Social Democrat leader in Bonn, drew considerable attention in Europe when he openly declared that the big companies collaborated in actions designed to destroy the small independent dealers in Europe also."

"What was the number of bankruptcies in America last year?"

"I believe they were listed at about 178,000."

"Do you know what is predicted for this year?"

"I've seen some figures that ran as high as 200,000."

The Bankers' Woes

"How many businesses that have gone bankrupt in recent years could have been saved by a bank loan that would have been available when money was more plentiful? I can remember only a few years ago when private banks were reported to have cash on hand in excess of fifty percent of the depositors' money. But as the value of money dwindled with inflation and the demand for loans increased, the reserves in many smaller banks fell as low as ten percent, and even six percent. In lieu of this disturbing situation, *U.S. News and World Report* asked, **Troubled Banks: What Is Being Done to Bolster Them?** The writer went on to state that 'The whole banking structure may be in trouble.' "

"Do you believe that?"

"Not altogether. Even when I was a youngster, Craig Hazelwood, president of the American Banking Association, said that one percent of the American banks controlled seventy-five percent of the nation's commercial deposits. (*Trade Fallacies* by Arthur Kitson, P.S. King and Sons, Ltd. Orchard House, W. London). And recently Paul Steiger said, "The biggest and strongest banks have developed a significant advantage. . . . It's time to show some sympathy to your friendly banker. For one thing he probably needs it" (*Los Angeles Times*, Aug. 19, 1971).

"So," added Joe, "the problems facing the small banks do not affect the big giants?"

"From an overall view of the situation, Joe, it seems more and more apparent that the day is rapidly approaching when the smaller banks and lending institutions will be forced to surrender most of their rights to the largest banks. I noticed in the San Diego paper, an article quoting Dr. Tibor Rosenbaum, who felt in several years there would be a socialization of all but the largest banks" (*San Diego Union*, April 29, 1973).

"And who is Tibor Rosenbaum?"

"He's with the International Credit Bank in Geneva, Switzerland, but some also say he is the banking brains behind such men as Dr. Wilhelm Hankel of the Hessiche Landesbank-Girozentrale of Frankfurt, which spreads its influence over several continents, and even behind the Iron Curtain."

"Lately," said Joe slowly, "I've noticed that the FDIC has been running large ads in the paper to the effect that they were now insuring the investors' deposits as much as $40,000. Are these ads intended to help calm the fears of those with deposits in smaller banks?"

"I would say so, and truthfully, the FDIC has cared pretty well for the depositors who have lost their savings in the five hundred banks which have failed in America over the past forty or more years. But those who know the total assets of the FDIC declare there would not be adequate funds to protect investors if there was a rash of bank failures simultaneously as there was in the 1930s. In recent times, we've seen the failure, for example, of the Franklin National in New York, and the San Diego U.S. National Bank. But this is a far cry from the 1352 bank failures of 1930, and the 2294 bank failures of 1931."

Afraid of Gold

"When Europeans in 1968 feared that their paper currencies could be cancelled," I continued, "they made such a rush to buy gold that two hundred tons of the precious metal were carried off by hoarders in one day.

"Americans, of course, were not among those who so feverishly bought gold, since it was against the law for them.

"But with the dawn of 1975 Americans could, for the first time in forty years, purchase twenty-four karat gold bullion. Many financiers, especially in Europe, predicted that the American people would rush to the banks and draw money from their savings in order to purchase large quantities of gold."

"But they didn't, did they?"

"No, thank God, they did not. If they had, you and I might pay for this lunch with something other than dollars. When I discussed this with a group of bankers in the East, they agreed that many small banks of the nation would not have had sufficient funds to supply customers in significant numbers who wished to draw from their savings large sums of money to purchase gold."

"So what would they do?"

"Close their doors. They would have no other recourse. When I mentioned this, in a public address, a man who had been with the Federal Reserve Bank for forty-three years, said, 'Sir, you are exactly right.' "

"I wonder," said Joe seriously, "if many people knew how

15

close we were to a banking crisis that could have eclipsed anything of the past?"

"It was dramatic to watch those days of January, 1975. Virginia Knauer, consumer advisor to the president, was quoted by the Associated Press as saying: 'Don't let gold dust blind your vision.' Some of the largest agents also ran ads which warned Americans against purchasing 'corrupt' gold. Such announcements may have somewhat deterred the public from buying gold in 1975, but I feel that more influential than anything else was a lingering memory of 1934. Even Charles Curly, a gold enthusiast, had to remind his readers that the government had called in all of the gold that year at the lowly price of $20.67 an ounce. Some men prominent in the fields of numismatics and economy have suggested that there could be a day in the future when the price of gold might fall to as low as $5.00 an ounce."

"Sounds impossible."

"True," I replied, "unless you know the history of the powers who control the pricing of gold. Incidentally, have you by chance read Richard Ney's book, *Wall Street Gang?*"

"No, I haven't, Willard. Tell me about it."

"He talks about the New York Stock Exchange and how its vast wealth and power are derived and maintained by keeping the investing public in uninformed confusion. He also claims that the Federal Reserve System and the European banking establishment contribute to the Exchange's almost unchecked power."

"That's pretty alarming talk. I'll make a note to pick a copy up and read it."

"Joe, do you remember a few days ago when the *Glendale Press* carried a headline reading: **Multi-Billion Dollar Institutions Leap into the Stock Market?** Beneath the headline, John Cunniff, Associated Press business analyst, said: 'Like a great weight dropped into a seesaw, the country's multi-billion dollar institutions leaped into the stock market this week, and bounced prices almost over the playground fence.' (*Glendale News Press*, January 30, 1975).

"So the stock market can be manipulated by those with sufficient power. An incident from Virginia Cowles' book, *The Rothschilds, A Family of Fortune, (p. 248)* that is most humorous, pertains to the sudden, unexpected drop in the value of stocks such as Royal Dutch Shell on the Paris Stock Exchange, the morning of June 30, 1949. Surprised brokers, fearing the worst, hurried to sell before prices fell further. Soon, however, prices resumed their normal stability. The mystery was explained when the press carried the announcement that the eighty-one-year-old Baron Edouard de Rothschild had died.

"The tax on the dead man's investments would be based on closing prices quoted the day of his death. So, Royal Dutch Shell, Rio Tinto, LeNickel, the Diamond Trust of Debeers, and other companies in which the Baron had invested, experienced sharp stock price decreases the day before his decease, and rose the day after the funeral. Taxes were paid on the Baron's estate accordingly.

Fear of Devalued Currencies

"Speaking of France, we were there in 1968, when the IMF introduced paper gold. The year before I had attended the International Board of Trade in New York, and listened to the thousand delegates from a hundred nations struggle with the problem of striving to carry on an increasing volume of world trade with an inadequate supply of currencies and credits.

"So the IMF decided to create money with a stroke of the pen. They announced that this new system was only for use in international trade, but some Europeans were skeptical. They claimed to have heard secret talks which indicated that this new system of S.D.R.'s, or "drawing rights," would soon be imposed on every private citizen. Some feared their paper money might be cancelled without warning."

"You can't blame them for being more apprehensive than we in America," answered Joe. "The Germans, for example, could remember going to bed on a Saturday night reassured by their government that their inflated money was safe. They awakened Sunday morning to read in the press it had been cancelled."

"That was in June of 1948, wasn't it?"

"Right. Were you there?"

"No, I came to Germany shortly after this happened, but I do remember reading in the *Stars and Stripes*, the official paper of the Army, about the rash of suicides that followed that announcement. It was sad. "But a moment in Europe even more vivid to my memory came in August of 1971, when the banks of Europe refused to accept American dollars from the 11th to the 18th. It was awfully embarrassing and awkward for thousands of tourists who could not get proper exchange for their dollars."

"Were you caught in that same plight?"

"No. Some weeks before, I was with with a Swiss financier who told me that this was coming, and advised me to change money sufficient to care for my family through those days."

"Did other bankers give similar advice to resident Americans?"

"No. In fact, I recall asking some bankers before August 11th what they thought about my friend's prediction. They treated it humorously, as though such could not happen."

"Then how did your friend know?"

"I never asked him Joe, but I suppose it is not too hard to explain. The U.S.A. devalued the dollar by eight percent that year. American exporters gained an advantage because they could sell their products at discounted value. But people in Europe who held American dollars began to mistrust our currency, which they had previously considered safe from such devaluation."

"To oversimplify one might say that any devaluation is a form of bankruptcy. It inevitably elicits a reaction from people who seek to protect their own interests in the international markets. In 1973, when we devalued the dollar another ten percent, this caused men such as Donald Platten, of the New York Chemical Bank, to tell a Senate subcommittee: 'If we do not begin to rebuild an efficient international payment mechanism, we can be certain that expansion of world trade and investment will begin to grind to a halt . . . and should this happen we might soon see the beginning of a world-wide deflation that could eventually make the Great Depression seem like a summer festival' " (*Newsweek*, March 26, 1975).

From Crisis to Crisis

"The nations of the European Common Market viewed with alarm the weakness of the American dollar in the early seventies, but they soon were forced to look at themselves. 'The British pound was being badly battered with no end in sight, and speculators started taking aim at the French franc. In Italy the government launched an elastic defense to maintain the value of its beleaguered lira . . . was it the beginning of a full-scale crisis?' " (*Newsweek*, March 22, 1976).

"Interesting," said Joe, reaching for his brief case. "You've mentioned that some doctors believe cancer is caused in part by fear. And I guess we've seen how fear has touched the old and the young, the housewife and businessman, farmer and banker, rich and poor—almost everyone. Their fears stem from one source, money."

"I should have added that there are senators and presidents who have expressed their fears that money masters are drawing us into a world government that no single nation will be able to control."

"It certainly makes the individual seem helpless to cope with these super powers," replied my friend, sorting through some papers which required signatures.

The Fear of Losing Freedom

"And this, Joe, is probably the very root of all of the fears. Born in the heart of every man is a great longing to be free, and today men see themselves rapidly losing their individual rights and the privilege of charting their own course for the future. This undoubtedly is man's greatest fear."

Handing Joe his pen and the signed papers, I said, "We may not see as much of you now that you have completed the building of our home and the studios on Broadway."

"We must get together again before long and finish our conversation."

"I doubt if we could finish it this week or this month," I replied with a smile. "Without question we are living in the most momentous hours of human history, as we are witnessing the dying of old systems, and the formation of the new. For several decades we have watched the super powers steadily increasing their scope of influence. We are now entering the dramatic time when these powers in the world arena will be locked in a final struggle for complete control." Reaching for the luncheon check, I found that Joe, as usual, had moved more quickly, and already had it in his hand.

"Next time," I said reprovingly, "I'll pay the bill."

"With what?" asked Joe with a laugh.

Chapter 2
Money Power

From our home on the hill, I looked down on the city and the freeways which were growing congested in the evening traffic.

"It will take more than an hour for Joe to reach Newport Beach at this time of day," I said to my wife, Verna.

"You know," I added, "if it had not been for Joe, you and I might still call Washington home."

"Home?" answered my wife, with an expression that caused me to burst into laughter.

"I guess a month or two in the year spent in this restful place hardly justifies calling it home," I replied. "When we moved here two years ago, I planned to restrict our travels so that we could relax and write. But in spite of my sincere intentions, the schedule of the past year or two shows more foreign travel than any past period of our lives."

In a more tender tone, I added, "It hasn't been too easy at times for you, has it, Verna?"

"Nor has it been monotonous," she added cheerfully, turning to the kitchen.

"No need for sympathy there," I said, as I moved toward the study. "She has enjoyed life as much as I."

Alone in my study, I reflected that all economic thinkers could be divided into two classes. Those who favor a world government, and those who oppose it.

But all of them agreed on one point, *money is power*. Karl Marx wrote, "Money plays the largest part in determining the course of history." And Gerald Ford, according to Robert Winter-Berger, said: "Money is the name of the game." Maybe, I thought with a smile, he had been nicknamed "Honest Gerry Ford" because he conceded the crucial role that money plays in government.

The struggle between legislators and bankers is as old as history. Benjamin Franklin acknowledged that men in government did not always understand the "science" of money. Over two centuries ago, he said, "We are still in the dark on money and most acts of Congress on the subject show the ignorance of that science" (*The Story of our Money* by Olive Cushing Dwinell, Forum Publishing Co., Boston.

Thomas Jefferson spoke of: "Moneyed corporations which already dared to challenge our government to a trial of strength" (Dwinell, p. 80).

Regarding the financiers of his time, Andrew Jackson declared: "I have no hesitation to say if they can recharter the bank . . . they will rule the nation" (Dwinell, p. 98).

James Garfield said: "He who controls the money of a nation controls the nation" (*Chronological History of Money* by Wickcliffe B. Vennard Sr., Omni Publication, Hawthorne, Califonia).

Teddy Roosevelt warned that the nation should be "protected from domination or manipulation of Wall Street" (Dwinell, p. 185).

And President Wilson said: "Don't deceive yourselves for a moment as to the power of the great interests which now dominate our development. They are so great that it is almost an open question whether the government of the United States can dominate them or not" (Dwinell, p. 190).

Apparently Woodrow Wilson doubted the success of his administration in controlling the money interests. For he also said: "The government of the United States at the present time is the foster child of special interests—the big bankers—the big manufacturers—the big masters of commerce" (*Who Runs the Congress* by Mark Green, James Fallows and David Zwick).

In speaking of the big money interests, I asked myself, "How big is big?"

According to some reports on John D. Rockefeller, his oil trusts increased in value from $40 million in 1882, to $200 million in 1896, to $800 million in 1914.

The Rockefellers of our day control three of the seven largest oil companies in America, and Standard Oil of New Jersey controls an additional three hundred twenty-one companies, according to *American Opinion* (p. 15, February 1974).

In seeking positions in government, the Rockefellers, according to George Thayer, had spent $60 million on political campaigns. The cost of conducting successful campaigns has increased through the years. Time on radio and television, space in papers and on billboards, and a hundred other costs, make any major seat in government a costly office to seek. Even Robert Kennedy, whose family reportedly spent $14 million on campaigns, said: "We are in the danger of creating a situation in which our candidates must be chosen from the rich" (*Who Shakes the Money Tree?* by George Thayer).

Money not only plays an important part in the campaign itself, behind the scenes it also wields a great influence in the life of candidates who enter the political arena through such organizations as the Council on Foreign Relations.

The Council on Foreign Relations

Through the years, I have listened to both praise and denunciation of the C.F.R. While some feel that the Council, with its membership of 1400 trained men, could offer valuable assistance to those in government facing complex problems of the space age, others complain that a philosophy favoring a world government predominates in the Council.

The critics contend that the Council is supported by financial powers of the nation which favors a world government and casts its influence over both the Council and subsequently the U.S. government as well. During one period, it was said that ninety percent of those in the administration had been associated with the C.F.R.

Men entering politics or who are otherwise active in government are seldom free from the influence of money. If political candidates do not have personal fortunes to finance their campaigns, they often have to depend on gifts from others. Legitimate as such gifts might be, the victorious candidate is frequently in the awkward position of facing the representative of a former donor seeking some favor.

The Lobbyists

It was only after we had lived in the Washington area for a time that I began to really discover the part lobbyists play in influencing the policies of the government. Many lobbyists are ex-congressmen and ex-senators who failed to win reelection. They have lifetime visiting privileges on the floor of the house they served. They also have a full knowledge of the intricacies of congressional bargaining, and a first-name acquaintance with many of the men active in government. At one time, more than 120 ex-congressmen and ex-senators were registered in Washington as lobbyists. Most lobbyists receive high salaries from the powerful interests they represent. The large oil companies and Eastern banks are especially well represented by their lobbyists on Capitol Hill.

When Wright Patman (D.-Tex.), who for so many years served as chairman of the house banking and currency committee, was removed from office, the press explained that "Patman has long been known for his attacks on big New York banks and the Federal Reserve Board . . . he attributed his defeat in Washington to lobbying by the big banks" (*Los Angeles Times*, January 23, 1975).

The Master Minds

If the issues at stake were not so important, the story of the development of the Federal Reserve Bank would be highly entertaining. Writers of fiction could not create a more colorful beginning than that described by B.C. Forbes, in his article, "The Men Who Are Making America." Forbes tells of Nelson Aldrich, the maternal grandfather of Nelson Rockefeller, and his secret meeting at a hunting lodge on Jekyll Island, off the coast of Georgia, with some of the most brilliant bankers of the day.

Regarding Nelson Aldrich, one writer states: "Senator Aldrich led on tariff and financial matters because he understood them by tireless study, therefore he was master of other men who had not paid the price of knowledge" (*Jewish Influences in America*, Vol. 3, Dearborn Publishing Co., 1921).

While Senator Aldrich surrounded himself with such bankers and brains as Henry P. Davidson of J.P. Morgan and Co., Frank A. Vanderlip, President of National City Bank, and A. Piatt Andrew, Assistant Secretary of the Treasury, the man who wielded most influence over Aldrich and the others and who was credited with being the chief architect of the Federal Reserve, was Paul Warburg of Hamburg, Germany (Vennard, p. 105).

Paul Warburg had grown up in his father's banking house in Hamburg. The bank, like the Rothschilds', dated back to the late eighteenth century. He had lived later in England

and in France where he served the Russian Bank for Foreign Trade which had an agency in Paris. After going to India, Japan and China, Mr. Warburg came to America, where he became keenly interested in the banking policies of the nation (*Jewish Influences in America, Vol. 3*).

Picking up a copy of *The Federal Reserve Bank* by H.S. Kenan, I turned to the section containing Louis McFadden's speech of June 10, 1932, to the Senate. McFadden was chairman of the Senate's Banking and Currency Committee and he regarded Paul Warburg as "one of the most ardent propagandists—and financiers of world government in the U.S.A." (Vennard, *Conquest or Consent*, p. 12).

In his address to the Senate, Mr. McFadden said, "Mr. Chairman, when the Federal Reserve Act was passed, the people of the United States did not perceive that a world system was being set up . . . that Russia was destined to supply man power and this country was to supply financial power to a superstate . . . a superstate controlled by international bankers and international industrialists, acting together to enslave the world for their pleasure" (Kenan, p. 20).

"Strong words," I said aloud. "Very strong." Could they be true? Eighteen years after McFadden's famous speech to the Senate, James Warburg, the son of Paul Warburg, addressed the Senate on Feb. 17, 1950, and announced "You will have world government. The only question is whether it will be by conquest or consent" (Vennard, *Conquest or Consent* p. 12). Would it be a world government, as McFadden had said, in which Russia was destined to supply the manpower, and America . . . the financial power?

American Bankers in Moscow

With the "money-crunch" of the early 70s causing thousands of bankruptcies in the U.S.A., John Wallach, writing in the *San Francisco Examiner* on April 17, 1975, asked a question that should provoke serious thought. He asked "Why had American bankers, like David Rockefeller, chairman of Chase Manhattan, gone to Moscow to open the first representative office of an American financial institution that Russia had had in fifty years?" Stephen Broening, who had accompanied David Rockefeller to Russia, wrote: "I arrived in Moscow on April Fool's Day, 1973. Chase Manhattan can't cash your check; The Bank of America can't accept your deposit, and Citibank can't help you with your second mortgage . . . but [we] are giving nine digit credit to the Russians." How could Mr. Brunst of First National City Bank of New York, and Mr. Yankovitch of the Bank of America, explain these Russian loans to those Americans who were crying for loans at home?

Were the loans to the Russians more profitable? Phyllis Schlafely apparently did not think so, for she wrote in the *Los Angeles Times* (February 18, 1974): "On loans where Americans pay as much as 11% Russians get the money from the American bankers at 6%." She also noted that "After putting up only 10%, the Russians get loans for almost twice the length of time that is often allowed Americans."

One might surmise that the Russians gave us better security. Henry J. Taylor didn't think so. He wrote in the *Memphis Press-Scimitar* that "The Soviet Union owes U.S. taxpayers $2.6 billion net. First, the U.S.S.R. knocked off nearly $2 billion. . . . It offered only $772 million. . . . The $772 million became $48 million" (March 16, 1976).

We should also ask if the loans were to feed the hungry? In spite of the fact that the Soviet Union is as big as the continent of South America, with twenty-six percent of its labor force engaged in agriculture, she came to America, where slightly less than three-and-a-half percent of the nation's man power works in agriculture, and asked America for a billion dollars' worth of wheat to feed her hungry.

The Russians were given $300 million and loaned $700 million at low interest to procure the wheat, for which they were charged $1.65 per bushel. Then she offered to sell the same back to America for $4.65 per bushel. This perturbed even moderate Senator Mansfield sufficiently to denounce the fraudulant action on a national television program.

The Red Carpet

When Murray Seeger saw the Russians giving the American bankers the red-carpet treatment in Moscow, he wrote (in the *Los Angeles Times*) about the irony of Communists thus greeting their ideological opposites. Murray reminded his readers that "Since the Soviet ruble has no value outside the country's border, all Soviet transactions with the Free World must be conducted with other currencies."

Furthermore, for Russia to keep pace with progress, she must have computers. To get them she would have to look to Western Europe or America, but even the Western Europeans acknowledged that America was responsible for eighty percent of their computer program. After the Soviet computer specialist, Alexander Lerner, dined with Congressman James H. Scheuer (Dem., New York), Mr. Scheuer reported that the Russians intended to purchase upwards of 15,000 computers from America or Western Europe over the coming fifty or sixty months. By March 1st of 1976, *Newsweek* magazine estimated that the U.S. was presently using 170,000 computers, while the Russians were using only about 15,000.

On a recent visit to Austria, I learned of a little-publicized meeting of the International Institute for Applied Systems Analysis at Schloss Laxenburg, near Vienna. Computer specialists from fourteen nations were there. The meeting was chaired by Kosygin's son-in-law, Jermen Gvishiani, and directed by Dr. Howard Raiffa of Harvard. Again it seemed that America was willing to provide the Russians with technology as well as money.

The Cause for Alarm

The complaints over the Russian wheat deal were mild, and the $80 million loan to Russia for the building of the world's biggest truck factory on the Kama River east of Moscow was virtually unnoticed. If the Russians needed wheat for food, or trucks and computers for peaceful use, there was no need for alarm.

But in a world that was spending almost $1 billion daily on armaments, many Americans were becoming more concerned about Russia's military strength. Is Russia's Military Might Superior? Under a bold heading entitled, **Is America No. 2?** *Newsweek* on March 1st, 1976, printed in a red panel, a table entitled, "The Military Balance," which read:

	U.S.	U.S.S.R.
Armed Forces	2,084,350	4,412,000
Tanks	10,000	42,000
Strategic Missiles	1,710	2,378
Megatonnage	4,000	10,000
Strategic Aircraft	463	135
Tactical Aircraft	8,500	6,100
Major Combat Ships	182	226
Aircraft Carriers	14	1
Missile Submarines	41	73
Attack Submarines	73	253

Out of the ten classifications of military strength, America led in only three, while the Soviet Union outnumbered America in seven departments.

Newsweek observed, "With 2,900 fighter bombers and 19,000 tanks, the Russians and their Warsaw Pact allies are geared for an east-west blitzkrieg . . . that would aim to break up Nato armies and sever their supply lines. Against that challenge, Western defenses look thin" (p. 15). In addressing Nato leaders in Brussels, Admiral of the British Fleet, Sir Peter Hill Norton, Chairman of NATO's military committee, declared: "Moscow remains committed to the goal of becoming the world's predominant power" (*Los Angeles Times*, December 10, 1975). U.S. Airforce General George S. Brown said: "We are greatly concerned about adverse military trends and what they portend for the future." And he added: "War does not have a rational beginning and we must be aware that the Soviet Union is developing forces to win" (*Newsweek*, March 1, 1976).

If these fears are founded on facts, then it would seem justifiable to ask why American bankers in Moscow give the Russians favored nation treatment with loans on better terms than what they offer to their own nation? Was it possible that our money men in Moscow were ignorant of Russian goals? Or were they, as some have charged, sympathetic to the idea that the money master of the world should be a *red* master?

"Supposing," I asked myself, "we should have a world government with a ruler like Karl Marx?" The thought was disturbing, but I dared to consider it.

Chapter 3
A Red Master

Early in life I had read the writings of Karl Marx. "How much has happened in the world since my youth," I thought, as I turned to reference books on Communism. Since World War II there have been half-a-hundred wars and rebellions over the world, but the majority of these have been brother fighting brother within the boundaries of a nation. In contrast to past history, when nation fought nation, today the world's battle lines are drawn more frequently over issues of ideology. Korea was divided north and south, and Germany east and west.

When our sons at an early age wished to walk in the Tower of London, or view the changing of the Guard, I found my mind frequently turning to Karl Marx, who had done much of his writing in the British Museum which contained the world's greatest collection of books and manuscripts in its famous library.

If his teachings were greatly responsible for the internal struggles of many nations, what kind of a world would we have if Marx were alive, and its master? As a student, Marx had been expelled from the University of Berlin, and had proven undesirable both in France and Belgium. As a husband, he failed to provide for his wife and family. His wife, Jenny von Westphalen, wrote "Let me describe only one day of this life as it actually was . . . one day the landlady suddenly appeared, since we could not pay the sum of five pounds we had to leave. It was cold and rainy, and I quickly sold all the bedding in order to settle accounts" (*Karl Marx*, by Otto Ruhle, p. 383).

His family seemed doomed to tragedy. His daughter, Eleanor, committed suicide. Laura, a second daughter, along with her husband, also committed suicide. A year after his wife died of cancer, his favorite daughter, Jenny, also died.

Another record reports that "When the financial destitution of the family was brightened by a gift of one hundred and sixty pounds from an uncle in Holland, Marx, instead of caring for the needs of his family, spent it on a spree with friends" (*Naked Capitalist*, by Cleon Skousen, p. 22).

As a manager, Otto Ruhle writes: "He was always in debt, . . . half his goods were always in the pawnship" (p. 383). As a laborer, Ruhle adds: "Conventional work put him out of humor" (p. 383). As a personality, Bakunin says: "Marx was egotistical to the point of insanity" (Skousen, p. 28).

A Mixture of Old and New

Marx built up a complicated theory of past and future history. He believed that all history is a history of class struggle. The chief sources of Marx's ideas were the idealism of Hegel and materialism of the ancient Greeks as expressed by Democritus. He also drew from others like the English economist, Ricardo.

Why did this man appeal to the masses? Because he promised to remake a world that would satisfy humanity's two great needs, universal peace and universal prosperity.

Marx reasoned that all evils could be traced to one root,

private property. If somehow private property could be eliminated, then class struggle would cease and the state would no longer be necessary. Marx's formula for remaking the world was, and is, cruel and ruthless. All who stood in the way of its implementation would have to be destroyed. Problems arising from marriage and home and family would be solved by doing away with marriage, home and family. Problems connected with money and markets would be solved by doing away with the same. Problems pertaining to religion would be solved by doing away with religion. Could Western bankers support a world government under a man who declared his two great goals in life were to dethrone God and destroy capitalism? The answer to that question is probably worse than ironic.

The Mistakes of Marx

Marx reasoned that property owners would grow richer and fewer, while the laborers would grow poorer and more numerous. Eventually the working masses would rise up in their wrath and sweep away their masters in a violent revolution. According to his theories, the revolution would break first in most advanced industrial countries.

Here, he was totally wrong. In spite of his so-called brilliance, his reasoning on this point was totally lacking in logic. A man with rather simple logic could see that the manufacturers of goods would be at a loss to dispose of the same if the masses of working people were too poor to purchase what they manufactured. As the workman prospered, he could bring comparable prosperity to the manufacturer who made the goods that he bought. So revolution did not break in the places nor in the manner he had predicted. It came first in Russia.

In studying the wars of past history, we must examine not only the immediate causes, but the underlying causes. There had to be a reason why Communism, which Marx predicted would come first to Western Europe, came instead to Russia. In searching for the underlying cause of that, one should probably go back as far as Ivan the Terrible.

Ivan the Terrible

Ivan the Terrible was actually the first to take the title of Tsar of all of Russia. Tsar, of course, deriving from the Latin *Caesar*. Prior to this, rival leaders from the principalities of Novgorod, Kiev, and Moscow, struggled for leadership, and then there were a couple of centuries when the Mongols of Asia plundered, conquered, and taxed the people. But this stopped in 1547 when Ivan the Terrible came to power. The last years of his reign were years of terror. He massacred his opponents and even killed one of his own sons in a fit of rage. After the death of Ivan, there followed thirty years of war and disorder. The Poles occupied Moscow, the Swedes Novgorod, and the Russian people seemed filled with despair.

The Romanoffs and the Revolution

Finally the Russians rose up and drove out the invaders and Michael Romanoff was elected Tsar by a national assembly of the people. The Romanoffs ruled from the year 1613 until 1917 when Tsar Nicholas abdicated in favor of a republic, and was later murdered. That was the end of the Romanoff's rule, and the end of the Tsars.

While visiting the Peace Palace in The Hague, I was reminded that it was Tsar Nicholas II who actually took the initiative in 1899 to invite the leading nations of the world to meet for a Peace Conference in The Hague. Twenty-six nations were represented at that first meeting in Holland, and forty-four attended the second peace meeting in 1907. During the twenty-three years of his reign, he built the Trans-Siberian Railway, and seemed to make definite progress in producing iron, oil and coal, and textiles. But he was a ruler, and made some tragic mistakes.

The Tsar had a son suffering from hemophilia, and a self-styled holy man named Rasputin claimed he could heal him. Rasputin, a poor peasant, born in Siberia, was almost totally illiterate. But this religious fanatic held a tremendous influence over the Tsar and the Tsarina, and he undoubtedly contributed to their downfall. In disgrace, Nicholas II lost the two-year war with Japan in 1904-1905. He also failed to meet the demands of his own people asking for reforms, and they rose up in protest. In spite of mass arrests, imprisonments and executions, he could not stem the tide of revolt. The darkest blot on the record of Tsar Nicholas II is known as "Bloody Sunday." On January 22, 1905, a priest named Father Gabon led thousands of unarmed workers to the Tsar's Winter Palace, to present their peaceful petition. The marchers carried large pictures of Nicholas and lustily sang, "God save the Tsar!" The Tsar did not come out to welcome them. Instead he ordered his soldiers to open fire on the defenseless marchers, and they did, killing approximately five hundred, and wounding six times that number. This marked the beginning of the end for the Romanoffs. In July 1918, the Tsar and his family were shot.

With the removal of the Russian Tsar, the nation stood at the crossroads. The whole world watched to see which path she would follow. In my own search for fuller understanding of this important moment of Russian history, I read views expressed by Cleon Skousen.

Mr. Skousen, who had received his degree in Law at George Washington University, and who had served with the FBI, and taught in a university, seemed to write with both honesty and authority. Taking his book, *Naked Communist*, from the shelf in my library, I read again his comments concerning the overthrow of the Tsar, and the powers who took control immediately following:

"The most significant thing about the abdication of the Tsar and the setting up of the People's Provisional Government in Russia, is the simple historical fact that the Bolsheviks, or Communists, had practically nothing to do with it. This revolution had been initiated by the same kind of people as those who started the revolt against the Tsar in 1905. They represented Russia's best people: the liberal aristocrats, the intellectuals, the businessmen, the millions of peasants and the millions of workers. But the Bolshevik leaders were nowhere in sight. Lenin was in exile in Switzerland. Trotsky was in exile in New York, and Stalin was in prison in Siberia. Unfortunately, for their future propaganda, the Bolsheviks would never be able to take credit for the Revolution of 1917, which brought about the overthrow of the Tsar" (p. 112).

Immediately following the overthrow of the Tsar, a provisional government was set up. For the first time in Russian history, it seemed that the people had the prospects of a liberal democratic regime. Prince Lvov said, "Our generation finds itself in the happiest period of Russian history" (Skousen, p. 112). But this happiness was short-lived. The leaders of the provisional government who generously allowed Lenin to return from exile, learned that, upon his arrival in Russia, he denounced the provisional government and demanded that a Communist dictatorship be set up. And, when he failed to get his way by ballot, he resorted to force. "This," says Skousen, "sounded the death knell for democracy in Russia" (p. 115).

Laying Skousen's book aside, I asked myself, "What kind of a world would we have if Lenin were its master?"

If Lenin Were Master of the World?

At the London Conference in 1903, Lenin and Trotsky had differed on the path that should be followed for world revolution. Trotsky spoke in favor of a peaceful plan, while Lenin insisted it would be one of violence. Later, of course, the record shows that Trotsky accepted Lenin's views and joined with him in what became one of the bloodiest purges of human history.

In his essay, "How to Organize the Competition," Lenin spoke of the need for "Purging from the Russian land all kinds of harmful insects" (Lenin Sobrannye Sochineniya, *Collected Works*, fifth edition, vol. 35, p. 204). The "insects" included many teachers, priests, monks and nuns, and those who sang in church choirs. Lenin advised Gorky not to waste his energy whimpering over rotten intellectuals. (Lenin, *Works*, vol. 51, p. 49.)

Regarding peaceful coexistence, Lenin wrote: "We have not forgotten that war will return. While capitalism and socialism live side by side, one or the other will ultimately triumph" (*V.I. Lenin on Peaceful Coexistence*, Progress Publishers, Moscow, 1971, p. 68).

From the window of my hillside office in Glendale, I could look down upon the city, its library within walking distance of our home. Only a few weeks before, I had visited that library and examined magazines which were published in America in 1943. I discovered that some of America's most popular publications were filling their covers with the face of Lenin and acclaiming him "perhaps the greatest man of modern times." It made me wonder, if some Western bankers were favoring world government, and willing to give Russia "favored nation treatment," would they accept a world with Lenin as master? Or would they settle for Stalin? American magazines in 1943 also praised Stalin as that "well balanced and rarest of men."

Scientific Dictatorship and Joseph Stalin

Lenin declared that the "scientific concept of dictatorship" meant nothing more or less than "unlimited power resting directly on force, not limited by anything nor restrained by any laws or absolute rules" (*The KGB* by John Barron, Bantam Books). Men such as Stalin followed the teachings of

Lenin. His bloody purges and rule by force conformed to the concept of "scientific dictatorship" taught by Lenin.

"What kind of a world would we have today." I asked myself, "if Stalin were still alive and 'master of the world'?" As a youth, Stalin tried to kill his father. Like Marx and Lenin, he seemed to despise any authority that challenged his own will. Svetlana, his daughter, described him best, when she wrote: "Everything was oppressive . . . my mother's suicide was most eloquent testimony to the hopelessness of the situation. . . . with his accomplices, he turned the country into a prison, in which everyone with a breath of spirit and mind was being extinguished: a man who aroused fear and hatred in millions of men . . . this was my father" (*Only One More Year*, p. 142). In describing her father's death, his daughter said: "His final gesture was to glance around the room and raise his hand as though pointing to something above and bringing down a curse upon them all" (she was quoting Khrushchev, p. 320).

The colleagues who praised him in life denounced him after his death. In 1952, Khrushchev declared Stalin to be "the wise leader of our party and people." But in 1956, only four years later, when addressing a party convention, he described Stalin as "a murderer and a pathological liar . . . guilty of mass murder, who forged false evidence against his alleged enemies and deported whole populations" (recorded by the U.S. State Department, June 1956).

When addressing an audience in Washington, D.C., in the summer of 1975, Aleksandr Solzhenitsyn spoke of 15,000,000 peasants being sent off for extermination, 6,000,000 dying of starvation in the artificially created famine in the Ukraine in 1932 and 1933, and as many as 40,000 being executed in a single month (*U.S. News and World Report*, July 14, 1975). Such was life under Stalin.

When I read the first edition of Solzhenitsyn's book, *Gulag*

Archipelago, scenes were indelibly stamped on my mind that time would not erase. When leaving Russia he spoke of being delivered from "the belly of the dragon." I recalled his story of the half-literate stove maker who used to occupy his free time writing his name. When he had no blank paper, he used the newspaper. One day in the communal toilet, someone found a discarded newspaper on which the stove maker had written his name across the face of Stalin. This cost the poor man a ten-year sentence in a concentration camp (p. 75).

Solzhenitsyn mentioned another who received a similar sentence for not turning on his radio when Stalin was making a speech. And he told of the director of a paper factory who was arrested and sentenced for ten years. He had the effrontery to be the first to stop applauding after Stalin had given a speech (p. 70).

Women were cast into prison, not knowing the crimes for which they were being punished. And he mentioned some who received sentences for stealing two potatoes or a spool of thread. Tanya Khodkevich was imprisoned for ten years because she wrote a poem which included the verses: "You can pray *freely* but just so God alone can hear" (*Gulag*, p. 37).

Regarding his own arrest, for having made a careless remark about Stalin which was not complimentary, Solzhenitsyn said: "How could I answer them? I was forbidden to say a word" (p. 167).

Journalists from over the world, such as Alsop of America, Peter Reddaway of Britain, as well as many of the leading Russian intellectuals, acclaimed Solzhenitsyn "the conscience of Russia." On April 5, 1976, *Time* magazine carried an article which read: "In an enthusiastic telegram to the Freedom Foundation of Valley Forge, Pa., Ford said he was 'delighted' at the award of the foundation's American

Friendship Medal to the Nobel prizewinner." But, the article went on to say, "The president's pleasure might well have been diminished had he anticipated Solzhenitsyn's bitter attack on U.S. foreign policy . . . [in which the Russian asserted that] the West has made so many concessions recently, . . . that the 'Soviet Union does not even need nuclear arms; you can be taken with bare hands.' " The *Christian Science Monitor* called his speech a "time bomb" while the *Wall Street Journal* rated it "One of the most important pieces of TV journalism ever. . . ."

The more that Solzhenitsyn received recognition from the president and praise from journalists, the more Americans were confused by American bankers giving financial assistance to Russia. If they favored a world government, could they accept the Russian model with its KGB? What would our world be like if the KGB ruled it?

If the KGB Were Masters of the World

Few people outside Russia could pronounce *Komitet Gosudarstvennoy Bezopasnosti*, the full name of the infamous KGB. Noel Barber of the *London Daily Mail* calls it "the world's greatest spy machine." Of all that I had read on the KGB, no author seemed to cover the subject more accurately and fully than John Barron. In 1969, he went to Holbart Lewis, the president and executive editor of *Reader's Digest*, with the suggestion for his book, and Lewis authorized him to take advantage of the world-wide resources of the *Digest*. Barron tells how "The KGB watches all 41,595 miles of the Soviet Union's land and sea frontiers. People caught in unlawful flight are liable to penalties ranging from a year's imprisonment to death. Were the KGB to vanish, with it would evaporate the basic means of regulating Soviet thought, speech, and behavior; of controlling the arts, science, religion, education, the press, police, and military" (*The KGB*, p. 1).

A Red Master

David Binder wrote in the *International Herald Tribune* (June 4, 1975): "Detente is said to give the KGB more work at home and abroad. . . ." In describing the work of the estimated 420,000 employees, he mentioned 175,000 guards assigned to Russian frontiers. "No Western intelligence agency," declared Binder, "is known to have such pervasive power." According to the specialist interviewed by Binder, in KGB usage, the United States remains the "main adversary." The Soviet Union had 1,083 nationals working in the United States as diplomats and trade representatives, whereas ten years ago they had only 456. It is estimated that forty percent of the Soviet diplomats in the United States are full-time intelligence officers.

The average American, like people in general, is not too impressed with either the description or numbers quoted in describing the KGB men of Russia. One must have some personal contact to drive truth home to the heart. Like statistics on murder or suicide, one may read the figures with a sigh and shake of the head. How different it is when tragedy strikes closer home, and someone of the family suddenly is the victim!

It took a personal experience to arouse my concern over KGB's activities.

One bright summer day in the mountains of California, my path crossed that of a young Russian who had defected from the Soviet secret police. His name was Sergei Kourdakov. As I listened attentively to him telling of his past life with the KGB, I understood more fully what David Binder meant when he wrote in the *International Herald Tribune* (June 4, 1975): "The KGB has an elaborate apparatus for dealing with civilian dissidents, with subsections assigned to Jews, young people, intellectuals and religious figures."

Kourdakov had been assigned to the latter. The young Russian told of the brutality of the KGB in breaking up religious gatherings. Depressed over his association with the secret police, he sought to escape by going to sea. His story seemed stranger than fiction. And yet, I believed it to be true. The emotion displayed on his handsome face showed the sincerity of one who sought something better than a profession designed to suppress his fellow men. Little did I realize in the serene setting of the quiet mountain resort that Sergei Kourdakov was telling us his story on the very spot where he was marked for death.

Gentle breezes blew softly from the mountain lake, as he told of his attempt to gain asylum in Canada by jumping from his ship on the night of September 3, 1971. I had heard his story before on radio, and had read it in the press, but it was more impressive to hear it directly from his own lips. While in the radio room of the ship, Kourdakov learned of a message stating that a sister ship, the *Maria Ulyanova*, was to join their ship, the *Elagin*, and carry him back to Russia.

Kourdakov said he was determined that he would never go back to the Soviet Union where he had been raised as an orphan in a state-run home. His memories of Russia were both glorious and bitter. While attending school, he had appeared on Russian television as the number one Communist youth of his province. He told of his attending the naval academy and being chosen to supervise 1200 hand-picked cadets.

While at the naval academy, Kourdakov was urged to join the secret police to head a special squad which opposed and arrested Russian Christians who met secretly for worship. He told of leading over 150 such raids. He described some of the raids, telling how his band would often come upon the Christians suddenly, snatching their Bibles and beating them until blood ran freely.

It was such depressing memories that caused him to risk his life in the cold waters of the Pacific, rather than be taken back to Russia. The night of September 3rd was stormy and the officer in charge of the ship had his radio operator ask the Canadian authorities if they might seek shelter in the territorial waters. The ship was only two miles off the Canadian coast when Kourdakov plunged into the dark waters. Five hours later, in the shadows of the dawn, he staggered, exhausted, onto the beach. Later, in a Canadian hospital, he told of his joy in realizing that he was free; free from a life of fear; free from the haunting memories of the KGB; free to chart his own course, and plan his own life. But his freedom was short-lived! From Vancouver, he was taken by the authorities and placed in prison and later moved to another prison in Quebec City. Kosygin, he was told, was due to arrive in Canada to discuss trade agreements, and the young defector's presence must not be allowed to offend him.

While in the Quebec prison, Russian officials sought to persuade him to return to Russia voluntarily. "They would have taken me forcibly," said Kourdakov, "were it not for the influence and effort of one Canadian, Pat Burns."

To this point we had sat in silence, listening with rapt attention to the young Russian, who spoke with such sincerity. But when he mentioned Pat Burns, I interrupted impulsively, "Three cheers for Pat. When he first began his career on radio, I thought he was as rough and tough as the Canadian coast, but through the years he won a place in all of our hearts. He's a symbol of a true Canadian who longs to see all men free. Tell me," I asked, "how did Pat influence your release?"

"First of all," said Kourdakov, "Pat shared my story with his radio audience. Then, I understand, he phoned Ottawa and talked with the Honorable Mr. Winch, the representative for British Columbia in the Canadian Parliament. Mr. Winch apparently talked to Prime Minister Trudeau, and I was released."

Grateful not only to the people who had secured his release, but also to God, Kourdakov entered a church and knelt to pray. He had now joined those whom he had once persecuted.

We sat for an hour alone among the pines . . . but were we alone? When we said goodbye to Kourdakov and drove to San Jose, little did we realize that only a few days later we would see headlines announcing his death. A rather hazy account of his death left the reader uncertain as to whether it had been suicide or an accident.

"I'm afraid," I said to my wife, "that I'm not too impressed with this account. Sergei Kourdakov would not be the only KGB defector who has met an untimely death."

With the death of Kourdakov adding credence to the words of Solzhenitsyn, who was receiving more and more publicity in the Western world, fear of detente seemed to be increasing. In addition to Solzhenitsyn, Andrei Sakharov, a Nobel Peace Prize winner, and Andrei Amalrik, an author, are also warning of Russia's growing military strength. Both of them, like Solzhenitsyn, were expelled from the USSR.

Was the Russian desire for detente sincere?

I remembered that Lenin had said, "Peaceful coexistence is an agreement concerning war" (V.I. Lenin, "On Peaceful Coexistence" *Articles and Speeches*, Progress Publishers, Moscow, 1971). In consideration of such a solemn statement, I turned again to the articles and speeches of Lenin that had been republished in Moscow in 1971, and continued to read: "We have not forgotten that war will return. While Capitalism and Socialism live side by side, they cannot live in peace; one or the other will ultimately triumph" (p. 68).

When Leonid Brezhnev was visiting the U.S.A., William Ryan wrote in the *Los Angeles Times* (June 21, 1973): "Brezhnev's visit to the U.S.A. follows the policy laid down by Lenin in 1920." *The Oregonian* (June 6, 1974) quoted Russia's minister of defense, Andrei Grechko, as saying that "detente must never be interpreted as slackening the ideological war which must go on so long as Capitalism exists."

Readers who reviewed Lenin's writings on peaceful coexistence found little comfort in such statements as: "This war will be to our advantage in every respect" ("Peaceful Coexistence," p. 69).

For several days I read and pondered these matters in the quiet atmosphere of my Glendale office. My study was interrupted one morning, however, when Verna laid the mail on my desk. "Wait," I said, as I noticed the top letter was from Brussels. "Let's see what George Flattery may have to say; it could be of interest."

"It is what I expected," I said, looking up at my wife. "George is asking if we will be in Brussels for the meeting with the leaders to discuss the work of the International Correspondence Institute."

"You don't have to tell me," she smiled. "I can see by your face that your answer will be 'yes.' "

"How long will it take you to get ready?"

"Ready?" replied Verna, with a laugh. "So long as I am married to you, I know better than to ever really unpack my cases."

"I must say," I added seriously, "that George's letter interrupts my writing at a most interesting place."

"And what is that?"

"A growing anxiety expressed by many in our nation concerning Russia's sincerity in detente. A lot of publicity lately is being given to the records of the arms race, and talk about Russian superiority. If America is becoming number two militarily, how can one explain the conduct of American bankers in Moscow giving more favorable financial aid to the

Russians than to Americans? Some writers are saying that our country is sailing in a fog and that its financial matters are famous for fuzziness.

"And Broening, who accompanied David Rockefeller to Moscow, purposely opened his article with the words: 'We arrived on April Fool's Day.' "

"And," inquired my wife, as she studied my desk covered with books and papers on money, "do you have an answer?"

"Yes," I replied, rising from my chair to take her hand in mine, "yes, I believe I do. And after our ICI meeting in Brussels, I will stay there and write it. I know of no question of greater importance at the moment, and there has to be an answer."

With that, Verna turned to the kitchen to make coffee, and I picked up the phone to call the travel agency with a request for tickets back to Brussels.

We chose an evening flight to Europe which would mean our arrival in Brussels would be mid-morning.

Even though the family no longer counted the crossings, there was still the spirit of anticipation that was evident each time I said, "We're going back to Brussels."

Chapter 4
The Struggle for Mastery

"This has to be one of the world's most beautiful cities," I said to my wife, as we drove in the sunshine through forest and parks, enroute to the city center of Brussels.

"With SHAPE, and NATO, and the Common Market all headquartered here, it has become an important place, too," added my wife.

"And don't forget banking," I added, with a smile. "Did you notice that the *Brussels Times* said Chase Manhattan of New York is seeking to buy Banque Bruxelles-Lambert's share of the Banque de Commerce?"

"Will it?"

"Probably. The article did say that the move is opposed by the Federal Reserve Board, but that 'in spite of the Board's action, Chase is planning to go ahead with their plans . . . with Chase increasing its participation to 80% by 1976 and the remainder by 1977 and 1978.' "

The article (April 16, 1976) also mentioned that Chase's

financial consulting and the marketing division in Brussels would move its operations to London. The reason for the move was thought to be "part of a general reorganization and centralization of operations."

The article would have left anyone with the impression that the Chase Manhattan Bank was more powerful than even the Federal Reserve. I recall a *Time* magazine article on Chase Manhattan Bank, which stated that the company had a globe-encircling string of 50,000 correspondent banking offices. The writer suggested David Rockefeller, chairman of the board, would be allied with men representing 100 billion dollars.

"If money is power, he's really got it, hasn't he?" remarked Verna, as we neared our destination.

"Yes," I answered. "I recall one writer speaking of David Rockefeller as 'one of that little group of men who sit at the financial hub of the world's wealthiest nation and by their nods give stop or go signs to enterprises from Bonn to Bangkok.' " (*American Opinion*, February 1974, p. 13).

"Many people believe he is in a position of greater real power than even the president of the United States. Isn't that so, Willard?"

"Verna," I said, "it would be difficult to prove he isn't."

Our conversation halted as we pulled up in front of our apartment building on Avenue d'Italie. Carrying the suitcases into the bedroom of the furnished apartment, I said to my wife, "After our meetings with International Correspondence Institute leaders, there'll be a temptation to spend time here in Europe with old friends, but I'm not leaving this apartment until I complete my manuscript."

That evening when dinner was finished, I said, "If the bankers lending money to Russia understand the true meaning of detente as described by Lenin, and the danger of Russia's military threat as expressed by General Brown, then logic would compel us to believe that if they are not sincerely Communists, they then must have a plan of their own for world government."

It does make sense of the facts, does it not?" asked Verna.

"As far as I'm concerned," I replied, "it is the only answer that makes sense, and I'll tell you why. America, like most of the world, is divided into the two philosophies, one favoring world government, and one opposing it. Through the years, I have tried to read the views of both parties. When I read Tom Paine's *Age of Reason* and Darwin's *Hypothesis*, and the *Manifesto* of Marx and Engels, it did not mean that I was accepting their arguments, but I did feel it was my duty to know why they wrote as they did. My faith in God and His Word was not weakened by reading the views of those who opposed Christianity; in fact, it was strengthened."

"Not everyone feels as you do."

"No," I answered with a smile. "I went into a bookstore which bore a sign "Patriotic Bookstore" and asked if they had a copy of Buckminster Fuller's book, *Utopia or Oblivion?* The saleslady looked at me with lifted eyebrows and said, 'Why, don't you know he is a Communist?' Apparently, she felt that anyone who favored a world government in any way was communistic. I am sure she was sincere, and I am equally sure she never read Fuller's book."

Buckminster Fuller was nominated for the Nobel Peace Prize in 1969. He believed that there was plenty of food to feed the hungry if the world could pool its technology and resources. But this would necessitate a form of world government. In *Utopia or Oblivion*, he says "I am completely convinced, for instance, that all humanity is swiftly tending to discard national identities and instead to become Worldians—nothing less" (p. 210).

To say, however, that this man is sympathetic to Communism would be wrong. Regarding the doctrines of Communism, he writes: ". . . the Communists say, what they are going to do is to make Communism universal and then the world will work. . . . The Communists say that they must kill off all the non-workers in order to make their system work. This is not a way of making the world work" (p. 243). Was it fair, I asked myself, to call a man like Fuller "un-American" because he expressed his concern for the world's hungry by urging international control?

Fuller did not believe that it was necessary for millions to be hungry. "We are operating," he wrote, "at an overall mechanical efficiency of only 4%. If we increase the overall mechanical efficiency to only 12%, we can take care of everybody" (p. 252).

Some who viewed the fallacies of the United Nations and its preponderance of Communist representation, felt that anyone who recognized this world organization was a Communist sympathizer. Sincere as such attitudes might be, they would hardly apply to everyone. Who, for example, would be less sympathetic with Communism's doctrines than Pope Paul who said, when addressing the U.N. in 1964, "this is man's last hope for concord and peace"?

If Buckminster Fuller with his anti-Communist remarks referred to a world system as a solution to feeding the hungry, and Pope Paul acknowledged the world governing influences of the U.N. as man's hope for peace, would it not be rational to think in a day of expanded world trade that some bankers would sincerely desire a world bank to insure stability for world trade?

The next morning after breakfast, I remarked to Verna, "We bought some groceries at the market up the street. Just for interest let's go into the kitchen and see where our food stuffs have come from."

For five or ten minutes, we were both fascinated to see that the butter had come from France, the eggs from Holland, the meat from Argentina, and the can of green beans from China. The can of salmon had been packed in Russia, and the grapefruit had come from Texas. The strawberries were from Casablanca, and the celery from Israel. Neither of us had realized, when loading our grocery basket, that this chain store market in Brussels stocked food from almost every corner of the world. "And," I added, "in any American city, a man may drive to work in a German Mercedes, or a Volkswagen, wearing an English topcoat and gloves made in Spain. At his office he may park his car between a Japanese Toyota and a Swedish Volvo."

Today multi-national companies representing billions of dollars move freely from one nation to another. In examining two hundred of America's top corporations, one report showed their foreign operations amounted to $8 billion in 1950, $20 billion by 1960, and $60 billion by 1970. Not only have American firms been expanding their interests to other lands, foreign companies have been doing the same in the U.S.A. Not long ago the Treasury Department revealed that 5,000 foreign-owned businesses in the U.S.A. showed a total book value of debt and equity of over $40 billion.

According to news reporter Shila Howard the assets of foreign banks in the U.S.A. have tripled in the past seven years.

In the *New Republic* magazine, "T.R.B." stated: "The top 500 corporations in America are virtually all global. And interlocking directorates tie them with the top dozen banks which are also nearly all global. International trade between nations is just as common as interstate trade was within the borders of the nation when it was young."

Although the founding fathers feared the power of a central bank, they nonetheless found it necessary. Today it seems that a world bank is also necessary. I recall hearing leaders of the Common Market some years ago stating their intentions and desires to see a one-world money system. The *Los Angeles Times* (February 4, 1974) reported that the

French were promoting a global bank. And I also recall a German newspaper, *Die Welt*, stating that "a one-world money system would automatically mean a one-world citizenship."

"So," I said, walking toward the window, "the circumstances of this day produce arguments both favoring a world money system and fearing it.

"Incidentally," I said turning to my wife, "do you remember, when we were here in Brussels in 1973, an article that appeared on the front page of the *International Herald Tribune* concerning eight institutions of America which own the controlling stock in 324 major companies of America?"

"With all that you collect on the subject," replied Verna with a laugh, "I'm afraid I'd hardly remember it."

"That article," I continued, "was quite significant. It was actually the report brought by Senate panels, under the leadership of Senators Muskie and Metcalf, which sought to investigate the leading financial powers in America.

"Morton Mintz, who wrote the article for the press, said that many of the big powers ignored the questions asked by the government, and others made irrelevant replies. But the 419-page report did reveal that the 324 top companies of America were controlled by eight financial institutions, six of which were banks.

"What interested me was the fact that Senate committees with all the backing of the American government had difficulty procuring a full report of the financial monopolies of America, which often plan their strategy in secret. I wonder if Senators Muskie or Metcalf were ever invited to a meeting of the Bilderbergers."

"A meeting of whom?" Verna inquired.

"They're a group of billionaires, educators, writers, and industrialists," I explained, "about 120 strong who first met together in 1954 in Bilderberg, Holland. They have continued to meet semi-annually since then. In 1971 they met in a Rockefeller-owned hotel in Woodstock, Vermont; in 1974 they came to the Rothschild ski report in Megeve, France."

"Beautiful country," said Verna, with a tone of voice that suggested that she was thinking more about the scenery than the Bilderbergers.

"True," I replied. "Baron Edmond de Rothschild's ski resort, Mont d'Arbois, is a beautiful spot for any meeting, but the French gendarmes made certain that no one got near the place while the meeting was in progress."

Interestingly, Prince Bernhard of the Netherlands has been a prominent Bilderberger since the group's inception. Some people have thought this strange alongside such names as Wallenberg, Rockefeller, and Rothschild. But one day I discovered that the Rothschilds had loaned money to the Russian czar in 1883, and in return had received oil concessions in Baku, Russia, large enough to make them competitors with the Rockefellers' Standard Oil Company. In 1911, they sold their oil interests to the Royal Dutch Shell Company.

Later, Victor Rothschild became advisor to the Royal Dutch Shell Company, and within six years Royal Dutch Shell had spread over twenty-eight countries with interests in five hundred companies. Queen Juliana of Holland was a chief shareholder in the Royal Dutch Shell Company, and thus I came to understand how her husband, Prince Bernhard, could be a leading Bilderberger.

Only One Power in Europe

But certainly, in continental Europe, one name stands out above all others in terms of fiscal power. That name is Rothschild. Prince Metternich said that the house of Rothschild played a larger role in French affairs than any foreign government except, perhaps, England (Cowles). French socialist Alexandre Weill actually said, "There is but one power in Europe and that is Rothschild" (Cowles, p 101).

When we were living on Avenue des Bleuets in Rhode St. Genese, I remember one day discussing with my older son, Lee, the part that money played in history. As we stood by the lion monument on the top of the mound overlooking the Waterloo battlefield, we discussed the terrible toll of the battle. From early childhood Lee had shown a keen interest in history.

I asked, "Can you tell me how many men Napoleon led into battle on that June 18th?"

"I believe it was 72,000."

"Right. And how many men did Wellington have?"

"Wasn't it 67,000?"

"Very good, and what were the losses?"

"The French lost 35,000 and the British 22,000."

"So far you rate a perfect score for your answers. Naturally you know that Wellington was victor, but who was responsible more than anyone else for that victory?"

"I'm afraid," said Lee, "you are going to have to help me with that question."

"There is no question, Lee, but that the one name most responsible for Wellington's victory was Rothschild. It is really a fantastic story. Would you like to hear it?"

Lee nodded, affirmatively.

"Before Wellington's men ever met Napoleon in Belgium, he and his troops were down in Spain in dire financial straits. He wrote to his government in Britain and asked that they be withdrawn.

"You see, his government had tried to send him gold on British ships, but they had been sunk or captured enroute. Nathan Rothschild had a plan which he believed would relieve Wellington's financial predicament. His scheme was like burglary in broad daylight. First of all, Nathan asked his father in Frankfurt to allow his nineteen-year-old brother, James, to go to France to work as a collaborator.

"The second step of strategy was to persuade the French that British gold should be allowed to reach France, which they suggested would be a sure method of weakening the British government by draining away her gold.

"So, the blockade was relaxed to the extent that a railed-off enclosure was apparently set up on the Channel at Grave Line, near Dunkirk, where some manufactured articles from Britain, and gold and silver, were allowed to enter France in a sort of legalized smuggling operation. But what the French did not know at that time was that James Rothschild, in following Nathan's instructions from Britain, had worked out a system to transport the British gold right across France and into Wellington's hands in Spain. While the French were priding themselves on draining away Britain's gold, they were actually cooperating in a Rothschild scheme to provide Wellington with the needed gold to care for his troops on the Continent, and, in the end, defeat Napoleon" (Cowles, p. 43).

Bank of England Bows to Nathan

One of the best stories about Nathan Rothschild concerns the Bank of England. One of the officers of the bank apparently refused to honor a Rothschild note at the same rate of exchange as a Bank of England note. The following day an angry Nathan made his way to the Bank of England, carrying a brief case filled with Bank of England notes that he personally possessed. Those were the days when Britain was on the gold standard, so Nathan had the right to demand gold in exchange for each of the notes which he presented one at a time to the bank clerk.

Throughout the day, Nathan continued to exchange his notes for gold. In seven hours he collected gold for 21,000 British pound-notes. But, that is not all. Nine of his representatives had been doing the same thing at other tellers' windows, which meant that the Bank of England lost 210,000 pounds worth of gold that day. And, as though that was not sufficient, he informed the bank that he had enough of their paper money to repeat the same process for a period of two months! The director of the bank called a hurried meeting and made favorable arrangements with Nathan. (Cowles, p. 60.)

When Nathan died, the *London Times* wrote: "The death of Nathan Mayer Rothschild is one of the most important events for this city, and perhaps for Europe, which has occurred for a long time. His financial transactions have pervaded the whole continent" (Cowles p.91.)

Fredric Norton said of the nineteenth-century Rothschilds, ". . . they conquered the world more thoroughly, more cunningly, and much more lastingly, than all the Caesars before them and all the Hitlers after them" (*The Rothschilds*, p. 21).

"What about the twentieth-century Rothschilds?" asked Verna.

"Jurate Kazickas," I answered, "wrote an Associated Press release that said, 'Rothschild money is spread today over six continents in more than 100 businesses in mining, oil, chemicals, tourism, food and banking.' And *Business Week* (January 12, 1976) devoted its cover to a colorful picture of the Rothschilds, and a five-page article entitled, 'The Rothschilds' New Power in International Banking.' "

Glancing at my watch, I realized that it was time to retire, and I moved toward the door saying, "The past history of 'money-power' is interesting, but the activities of present-day financiers is fascinating and awesome."

Crossroads of Europe

With the dawn of a new day, I stepped out on the balcony of our apartment and looked out across the city of Brussels.

It was hard to realize that a week had passed since we had arrived in the city. With amusement I watched a bird on the street pecking vigorously at its own reflection in the shiny hubcap of a car. The pattern of red-tiled roofs of the houses nestled comfortably among the trees was severely interrupted by the mechanical arms of the huge cranes dominating the skyline. As land became more precious the trend toward high-rise apartment dwellings continued.

Glancing down Avenue d'Italie, I could see Verna in the morning sunlight returning from Sarma's market with a bag of groceries. Although the market was still called Sarma's, J.C. Penney Company now owned this chain of food stores. But this was not unusual; the large department store in the heart of the city carried the name of Sears; and Hilton, Sheraton, Ramada, and Holiday Inn were familiar names in this crossroads of Europe. Daily the world seemed more international

Returning to my desk, I recalled a conversation I had had with a Belgian banker about international trends of the day. Like most Europeans, he reflected anxiety over Russia's military strength and ambition for world control. When I asked if he had any comment concerning American bankers lending money to Russia in these critical times, he merely replied, "Trying to build a better world, I suppose."

I picked up a copy of *Great Ideas Today 1971*. It was devoted primarily to the records of those seeking to build a better world with a one-world government. The impact of the atomic bombing of Hiroshima and Nagasaki prompted a petition to Robert M. Hutchins, Chancellor of the University of Chicago, to organize a committee to frame a world constitution.

This committee produced 4,500 pages of text. The preamble read: "Universal peace is the prerequisite of that goal . . . iniquity and war inseparably spring from the competitive anarchy of the national states; and therefore the age of the nations must end." (*Great Ideas Today, 1971*, p. 333).

I studied the contents of various chapters, "Ecology: A World Concern," "Toward a World University," "Prospects for a World Government," and so on. "Universal peace is the prerequisite," I repeated as I pushed the book aside.

The words of the world constitution committee were redolent of the charter of the United Nations, which read in part: "We the people of the United Nations determined . . . to save succeeding generations from the scourge of war . . . to live together in peace with one another as good neighbors. . . ."

"What high hopes they had," I said sadly. "And their beautiful document was only 405 days old when the bombs were dropped on Japan." My feelings were not unlike those I had when I first visited the Peace Palace in The Hague and learned that it had been dedicated August 28, 1913, only about a year before World War I erupted. It was a beautiful building, I recalled, with its statue of Andrew Carnegie, who gave $1,500,000 for the construction and upkeep of the Peace Palace. And, by the time of my visit, statues of Gandhi and Schweitzer also adorned its halls.

After the first war, men erected in Ariana Park in Geneva, buildings to house the League of Nations. The dedication of this world center on January 10, 1920, represented another effort to establish peace, but nineteen years later, the world was plunged into World War II, which was still raging in the South Pacific when the U.N. was born.

The colorful scenes in San Francisco which welcomed the first U.N. delegates were something I would never forget. But time had brought many changes in the U.N., and some of them had been stormy and unpleasant. There was the event of October, 1971, when TV cameras recorded the orgy of dancing on the floor of the General Assembly when

Nationalist China was expelled. U.S. Ambassador Bush said, "Never have I seen such hate." Three years later Yassir Arafat, the Palestinian terrorist leader, mounted the platform of the General Assembly with a pistol on his side, and spoke for ninety minutes. This was the same man who said, before coming to the U.N., "We shall never stop until Israel is destroyed. . . . Peace for us means the destruction of Israel, nothing else."

When he left the cheering Assembly, the Israeli delegate to the U.N. asked for the privilege to speak, and was not allowed a single word. In the meantime, Arafat's visit cost American taxpayers $750,000, because this nation is obliged to provide security for such visitors. When Ambassador Scali suggested to the U.N. that the American people were becoming weary of paying the bills for a body which was so disdainful of Israel, Bishara of Quwait called Scali's speech "an unappetizing mixture of tasteless ingredients." But if Scali's remonstrances seemed mild, other Americans soon spoke up more vigorously. One headline shouted **Hypocrisy in the U.N.** Senator Jackson accused the U.N. of political blackmail. Senator Humphrey said, "It is entirely possible that the U.N. in 1974 could be like the League of Nations in the 1930's . . . powerless and useless." Senator Goldwater said, "The U.N. is a forum far different from the one we envisioned and voted for in 1945. . . ."

Ambassadors have come and gone at the U.N., but the old problems remain. On January 26, 1976, *Time* magazine quoted Ambassador Moynihan as warning that the U.N. could become "an empty shell."

U.S. News and World Report (February 16, 1976) added another statement by the Ambassador who suggested that the U.N. General Assembly was becoming "a theater of the absurd."

One notable change in the U.N. since its founding has

been in the complexion of the General Assembly. It has almost tripled its original size and most of the new members represent underdeveloped, third world nations. When these representatives are united on an issue, they have a solid majority in the assembly. This happened, for example, when the assembly entertained a resolution decrying Zionism as a form of racism. It carried easily. Seventy-two members favored it, thirty-five opposed it, and thirty-two abstained. The USSR was among the few large industrial nations to support the measure—it was, in fact, a conspicuous promoter of it.

Israel's U.N. ambassador, Chaim Herzog, said the resolution was passed after two weeks of behind-the-scenes diplomatic wrangling and that it was an explicit act of anti-semitism, "the first organized international attack on Jewish religion since the Middle Ages" (*San Jose News* October 17, 1975).

With the U.N. divided by ideologies and its balances having changed so radically from the early days, what power would finally emerge strongest from this conglomerate of nations representing ninety-eight percent of the world's people? This was an important question, and I believed there was an answer.

No nation could survive without some form of money as a medium of exchange, and it was becoming more and more apparent that the present currencies of the world would soon be obsolete. When the leaders of the European Common Market were questioned about the future of the European currencies, they said emphatically that they would eventually be cancelled!

Some fiscal experts were predicting a new world money system, but could not agree as to when this might happen. However, they all said that if we did not soon establish the one-world system, we would face a catastrophe in world trade that would bring about a world-wide depression.

Special Drawing Rights

With the nations of the Western world running short of money, special drawing rights were introduced in 1968. While some said special drawing rights were to be used only in international trade, others maintained they eventually would be used by individuals also. This entire system, of course, would be associated with the United Nations. By the summer of 1975, the international airlines were working with the International Monetary Fund to work out a system of payment where international air travel could be paid with special drawing rights. The endless varieties of world currencies which changed in values from day to day were a nightmare of confusion.

When the price of petroleum quadrupled in 1973, the World Bank in report no. 447, paper no. 3, entitled "Prospects for Developing Countries," stated that, if the profit on oil continued at the present level, it would mean a $650 billion profit by 1980, and a $1,200 billion profit by 1985.

Although the pace of profit has apparently slackened to some degree, Eric Pace wrote in the *International Herald Tribune* (April 8, 1976) that Saudi Arabia cash holdings have doubled. H. John Witteveen, managing director of the International Monetary Fund (IMF), said, "The currencies surpluses earned by oil producers represented a staggering 'disequilibrium,'" and suggested that the IMF go out of its way to act as a clearing house.

But the influx of cash to the coffers of oil-producing Arab nations aroused the jealousy of the non-oil-producing Arabs, notably Egypt. The Egyptian press denounced their newly opulent cousins for depositing their money in the banks of "the invaders"—a phrase that likely alludes to the French and English occupation of the Suez Canal some years ago and perhaps also to Jewish European banking interests, since the Arabs regard the Jews as invaders of the Middle East.

However, the financial squeeze together with a growing disenchantment with the Soviet Union have produced an unlikely friendship between the Sadat government and the World Bank. Even stranger is the news that David Rockefeller has become an informal financial adviser to Anwar Sadat. The *Memphis Press-Scimitar* (March 23, 1976) article also reported that ". . . Mr. Rockefeller wanted to study the Egyptian economy more closely, and that Egypt would have to approach public sources of financing like the World Bank and the International Monetary Fund before being able to borrow from U.S. banks like Chase Manhattan."

The Birth of the World Bank

If world government increased its power, certainly Russian rubles would not serve a world system, nor would any other national currency. It would require a neutral system such as was instituted for special drawing rights by the IMF. With almost every nation of the world represented at the U.N., the IMF and the World Bank were becoming ever more meaningful.

"Is it possible." I asked myself aloud, "that brains of the banking world which met at Bretton Woods on July 1, 1944, had this long-range plan in mind when plans were made for the International Monetary Fund and the World Bank to help with reconstruction and development after the war?" They formed the IMF a year before the U.N. was organized. Could this have been in the mind of the Rockefellers who gave $8 million toward the purchase of the land for the U.N. headquarters in New York?

Once those headquarters buildings had been erected on

the banks of the East River, I asked Colonel Alfred Garr to join me in the production of a documentary film that would include the work of the United Nations. Through the years, he had assisted in the production of documentary films in Africa and India and China. After the bombing of Hiroshima, he had gone to Japan at our request to photograph the devastation of the atom bomb.

I remember the day we were to meet at the U.N. While I awaited the colonel's arrival, I had time to walk between 42nd and 48th Streets, and study the three major buildings of the U.N., which were spread for six blocks over an area of about eighteen acres. Inside the General Assembly building, was an auditorium half the size of a football field. As I paused by the beautiful fountain at the entrance of the Secretariat building, I admired the thirty-nine-story building of blue-green glass encased with aluminum and set in marble from Vermont.

While the colonel was busy with his photography on the outside, I entered the building and studied its appointments. The pendulum hanging from the ceiling seventy-five feet above my head was the gift of Holland. It represented a rotating world. Then there was the statue of Zeus, from Greece, and the nickel-silver doors from Canada.

When I stepped outside the U.N., I saw Colonel Garr was intent on photographing a marble slab which was a gift of the Soviet Union. I watched him move the camera slowly across the face of the slab on which were engraved the words: "And they shall beat their swords into plowshares, and their spears into pruninghooks: nation shall not lift up sword against nation, neither shall they learn war any more" (Isa. 2:4).

"That does it!" said the colonel. "We're all through! Bring the station wagon and we'll load the equipment."

Later that evening in the hotel dining room, the colonel

set his empty coffee cup down with a thud and asked, "Why in the world would the Russians give the United Nations a marble slab the size of the side of a house on which is chiseled a verse from the Bible?"

"There is something very subtle about that quotation on the marble slab. Did you notice it?" I replied.

"I noticed it was a verse from the Book of Isaiah."

"But," I continued, "did you notice that it was only half of a sentence?"

"No," replied the Colonel. "I really didn't."

"It makes a world of difference," I continued, "when you break a sentence. You may twist the meaning to imply the very opposite of what the writer meant to convey. Instead of commencing the sentence as Isaiah wrote it, the text in marble begins in the middle.

"The Communists chose the portion of the text promising a time of peace when the nations 'would know war no more,' but they infer it will come through a Communist-dominated organization. But Isaiah wrote about a peace that would come in *God's time and way*. He said: 'And he [the Lord] shall judge among the nations, and shall rebuke many people: and they shall beat their swords into plowshares, and their spears into pruninghooks: nation shall not lift up sword against nation, neither shall they learn war any more' (Isa. 2:4 complete).

"So," said the colonel, with a touch of anger, "the atheistic Soviet leaders chose a Bible passage predicting world peace and, by removing God from the text, suggested that they will bring that peace through the U.N."

"You know, colonel," I said thoughtfully, "that makes me remember what President Truman said, just about the time this slab was placed by the Russians at the U.N."

"What was it?"

"In a speech in Columbus, Ohio, on March 7, 1946, he said,

'O for an Isaiah or St. Paul to reawaken a sick world."

For a long moment neither of us spoke. Our minds were traveling back over the war years. The colonel finally broke the silence. "It does make a difference, when you've been there. When you've seen it and heard it and felt it. When you've breathed the very air of destruction and pushed on as in a daze, while shells scream overhead, while bombs burst beside you, and in front of you, and all around you. I saw the pride of yesterday's architects pulverized to dust. I remember when, suddenly, the roar and din of battle ceased, and all was silent. Well, almost silent! But I heard the crying of crazed children wandering through ruins in search of their parents. I saw them standing by the piles of bodies that soon would be pushed into mass graves and forgotten.

"As an officer I held my head high and bravely shouted orders, but inwardly I was crying, 'Dear God, is this man's only path to peace? Is there no other way?'

"In such an hour, you'd walk a second mile, or a second hundredth mile, with any one who would honestly seek a better path to peace. But in spite of the emotion that burnt in my heart, I knew that just as it takes two to make a fight, it takes two to make peace. I couldn't forget the pathetic sight of Prime Minister Neville Chamberlain beating his well-traveled road to Munich, thinking he had assured peace only to discover that he had played into Hitler's hands. Instead of peace we had Dunkirk, the Battle of Britain, El Alamein, Stalingrad, Pearl Harbor, Guam, Leyte, and Iwo Jima, and three-score millions dead, a baptism in blood and tears."

From the hotel entrance I watched the colonel enter a cab and head for the airport.

"What a man" I said, as I watched him go. He had been born in Hong Kong and was raised there by his missionary parents. In later youth he sang professionally with the best of Hollywood's tenors. He had won more medals than any soldier I knew, but deep in his heart he was as tender as a child. His youth camp in North Carolina was one of the finest in the nation, and his interest in others spread to all nations.

"What a man," I said again as I turned my thoughts toward current events and another day in Brussels.

Chapter 5
The Red Master's Defeat

I awakened one morning to the sound of planes overhead. For a moment I wondered where I was, but I quickly remembered I was in Brussels. In the earlier years of flying, we sometimes tried to guess the type of plane by the sound of the motor or motors. How many changes had come with time.

I remembered the beautiful Lockheed Constellations with their elegant curved fuselages. In 1953 I flew in one out of Calcutta. Its flight was interrupted by engine trouble and I spent some unscheduled time in Istanbul. Then came the Viscount turbo-jet. It was a British plane with propellers driven by jet turbines. I first flew on one on a trip to Athens. Now the new supersonic Concordes have virtually halved the time formerly required for long distance flights.

The aircraft this morning that were circling in the grey shadows of early dawn were helicopters; the staccato of their motors told us they were flying low. "Undoubtedly they are military," I thought, as I moved toward the window. Two years ago it was announced that the world was spending $247 billion on arms and armies, and this year the price of war machinery would cost the world more than $300 billion. One plane, the B-1 bomber, would cost America $72 million (*International Herald Tribune*, April 21, 1976).

Some of my friends have told me my meditations were at times too serious and that they chose to avoid such thoughts. For me it was not that easy. In a few days I was scheduled to speak in the military chapel at SHAPE headquarters, and scarcely a week passed in Brussels that we did not pass the NATO headquarters as we went to and from the airport.

In his last address at NATO, Sir Peter Hill-Norton, chairman of NATO's military committee, disclosed that during the previous spring, the Russians undertook for the first time a regular rotation of their combat troops in Eastern Europe by air, instead of by rail and road, and completed the movement in one-third the time of the old method (*Los Angeles Times*, December 10, 1975).

In discussing the military powers of the day and their potential for destruction, the Premier of Russia alluded to Armageddon, the biblical term for the last and bloodiest battle that man would fight. When Douglas MacArthur returned from the South Pacific, he said, "We are now entering Armageddon." When the American president signed the non-Proliferation Treaty, he said with a sigh, "This might defer Armageddon." When criticized for his action at the U.N., Adlai Stevenson replied, "Think of us as frustrated men on the verge of Armageddon." And the fiery ambassador, Patrick Moynihan, alluded to Armageddon frequently.

Several years had passed since I had been responsible for the production of a film entitled *The Drums of Armageddon*. I spent weeks that summer on the historical battlefields of Europe. I wept near Verdun, when I stood amidst 25,000 crosses and realized that man's history had been written with rivers of blood.

When and where would Armageddon be fought and, more important still, who would fight? And who would win? Only the prophets could answer. If the atmosphere of the United Nations seemed anything but peaceful, at least the slab of marble at the entrance bore the promise of the prophet, Isaiah, that following man's last great battle, peace would come.

Walking to the table, I took my Bible from the shelf and sat down to read. More than half a century had passed since my father read the Bible for the first time. Someone had placed a Bible in his hotel room, and he opened it randomly to words written by Isaiah and that spoke of peace. From that day on, the Bible became very much a part of his life, and also an important influence in the lives of the other members of the family.

In my youth, I was absorbed by history. The Bible, I discovered, was full of history and my absorption carried over in my earnest desire to read it. But it was strangely unlike my other history texts. An intriguingly prophetic note resounded throughout its pages so that it looked to the future as well as the past.

A Sure Word of Prophecy

Speaking of this prophetic note, the apostle Peter said: "We have also a more sure word of prophecy; whereunto ye do well that ye take heed . . ." (2 Pet. 1:19). Likewise, after Daniel the prophet had interpreted Nebuchadnezzar's dream about God's plan for the world's history and how various empires would rise and fall, he announced that "the dream is certain, and the interpretation thereof is sure" (Dan. 2:45).

Today many outstanding men consider the prophecies of the Bible to be accurate. Robert Morris Page, with many scientific awards and achievements, including his patents on pulsation radar, says: "The authenticity of the writings of the prophets is established by such things as the prediction of highly significant events far in the future" (*The Evidence of God in an Expanding Universe*, by John Clover Monsma, G.P. Putnam's Sons, p. 29).

Others of scientific reputation selected several prophecies of the Bible that pertained to the rise and fall of certain cities. They placed these predictions in computers with the question, could the fulfillment of these have been mere coincidence? The answer was no. But the questions placed in the computer represented only a very small percentage of the predictions of the Bible prophets, who discussed nations and kings which would come and go, and battles that would be lost and won.

Regarding Cities and Kings

In some of the world's greatest cities, like Babylon and Nineveh, prophets of God announced that they would pass away even while they were at the height of their power. But to lowly towns like Bethlehem they spoke of everlasting glory. And to beleaguered Jerusalem which stood in the path of advancing armies from the north and the south they spoke of restoration. Jerusalem experienced twenty-two sieges and heard the hammers of the builders in reconstruction eighteen times.

The Persian King, Cyrus, played an important role in his day in the rebuilding of Jerusalem and the temple. One hundred seventy-five years before he was born, the prophet, Isaiah, called him by name, and described his work. He wrote: "I have surnamed thee, though thou hast not known me" (45:4). And "[Cyrus] shall perform all my pleasure: even saying to Jerusalem, Thou shalt be built, and to the temple, Thy foundations shall be laid" (44:28).

Some students of prophecy have counted over forty kings that Bible prophets described before they arrived on their thrones and accomplished their works. When the apostle Paul stood as a prisoner before King Agrippa, he asked: "King Agrippa, believest thou the prophets? I know that thou believest" (Acts 26:2).

The Covenant with Abraham

God made a convenant with Abraham, the father of the Jewish race: "I will establish my covenant between me and thee and thy seed after thee in their generations for an everlasting covenant, to be a God unto thee, and to thy seed after thee. And I will give unto thee, and to thy seed after thee . . . all the land of Canaan, for an everlasting possession . . ." (Gen. 17:7, 8).

The prophets foresaw times when Israel would be driven from that land, but they also promised restoration. Moses declared: "If any of thine be driven out unto the outmost parts of heaven, from thence will the LORD thy God gather thee . . . And the Lord thy God will bring thee into the land which thy fathers possessed, and thou shalt possess it . . ." (Deut. 30:4, 5).

After four hundred years in Egyptian bondage, the people of Israel did return to the land that had been promised to the seed of Abraham. Around 720 B.C., the ten tribes of Israel were taken captive by the Assyrians, and one hundred twenty years later Judah was taken into exile by the Babylonians.

But they returned from Babylon; one group in 536 B.C., another under Ezra seventy-eight years later, and another group under Nehemiah fourteen years after that. In 63 B.C., the Jewish nation came under Roman rule. In A.D. 70, Jerusalem was destroyed by the armies of Titus and many were scattered abroad.

In A.D. 637, the Moslems took Jerusalem, and as time passed, successive invasions of Palestine brought the Seljuk Turks, Abbassides, and Fatimids. The European crusaders with all of their cruelty took control in 1099 but were driven out by Saladin in 1187. Richard the Lion-Hearted retook it in 1190, but the Moslems gained control again, and the Mamelukes of Egypt ruled from 1250 to 1517.

In 1517, the Turks captured Jerusalem and held it for four centuries. But, in spite of the many invaders, the people of Israel had actually ruled their land much longer than the Romans, Arabs, Crusaders, Mongols or Turks. Amos Elon, the Israeli correspondent for *Ha'aretz*, quoted El Khaldi, an Arab member of the Ottoman Parliament, who wrote to Rabbi Kahn of Paris, "Historically, it is your country" (*The Israelis*, Holt, Rinehart and Winston).

Even though the Jews had been driven from the land on numerous occasions, their prophets declared that they would return. Jeremiah wrote: "I will bring them again into their land" (16:15). Ezekiel declared: "I will even gather you from the people, and assemble you out of the countries where ye have been scattered, and I will give you the land of Israel" (11:17). Amos also brought the promise of God: "And I will bring again the captivity of my people of Israel. . . . And I will plant them upon their land, and they shall no more be pulled up out of their land which I have given them . . ." (9:14, 15).

Chaim Weizmann said: "God promised all of Palestine to the children of Israel" (Elon). Weizmann (1874-1952) was a Russian chemist who spent his early years as a teacher in Switzerland and England. His chemical research helped Britain's war effort (1914-1918) significantly, so much so that he was able to influence a grateful government to issue a declaration favoring "the establishment in Palestine of a national home for the Jewish people." It was called the Balfour Declaration after British foreign secretary, Sir Arthur James Balfour, who handed the document to the president of the British Zionist Federation, Lionel Walter de Rothschild, on November 2, 1917. Only a few weeks later

General Allenby's troops took Jerusalem from the Turks, who were then allied with Germany, and thus opened a way for the Zionists to make practical use of the Balfour Declaration.

Baron Edmond de Rothschild of Paris, more than any other single man, helped to finance Jewish immigration to Palestine. Before his death in 1934 his total contributions to the effort were estimated at ten million pounds (Elon).

Mayer Amschel Rothschild, Edmond's grandfather, was apparently a man who genuinely feared God. He and his wife, Gutle, raised their five sons to similarly reverence the Almighty. Amschel Mayer, the oldest son, was known to give himself to long periods of fasting and prayer; his younger brother, Nathan, Edmond's uncle, observed the holy days with serious devotion. Their father commenced his last will and testament with the words, "With the help of God. . . ."

Edmond was also a man of prayer. He even kept one room on his private yacht set aside only for prayer (Cowles, p. 183).

The 1335 Days

Many prophetic utterances of the Bible were fulfilled in that momentous year of 1917. One of the most intriguing was that of Daniel 12:12: "Blessed is he that waiteth, and cometh to the thousand three hundred and five and thirty days."

We have learned that, to properly understand such passages, we may need to equate days and years (see Numbers 14:34). In commenting on this verse, Gordon Lindsay suggested that the Mohammedan rule of Israel ended in 1917 in a peculiar fulfillment of it, since 1917 was the year 1335 on the Mohammedan calendar. He explained further, "It is interesting to note that until the year 1917, the Turks reckoned by . . . lunar time. Coins minted after that year no longer carried this reckoning."

Turkish coins minted that year bear both the dates 1917 and 1335 (Gordon Lindsay, *Israel's Destiny and Coming Deliverer*). "Blessed is he . . . that cometh to the thousand three hundred and five and thirty days."

A Reason for Loaning to Russia

As I pondered the part that Rothschild wealth played at the turn of the century in assisting the young colonies in Israel, I wondered if there could be some relationship between this and David Rockefeller loaning money to Russia.

On February 20, 1976, I had sat in the Brussels Hilton watching the arrival of Jews coming from thirty-two countries of the world. It was the Second World Conference on Soviet Jewry. In the Palais des Beaux-Arts, the audience heard Dr. Alexander Voronel tell how a Jew applying for permission to leave the Soviet might wait five weeks, five years, or forever. Three-quarters of a million Jews wished to leave the USSR. Statistical charts show that only a small fraction of these people have achieved their goal.

Table of Jewish Emigration from the USSR, 1971-75

1971	14,000
1972	31,000
1973	35,000
1974	20,000
1975	13,000

Anyone familiar with Russian history would understand why Jews would wish to leave. In speaking of the early life of Golda Meir, Amos Elon said: "She had vivid memories of the hammers boarding up the doors and windows and the clatter of the horses hoofs of the Cossacks who rode through the Jewish streets in Kiev, as they put their houses to the torch." Between 1881 and 1903 waves of anti-semitic pogroms swept from Warsaw to Odessa with "violence unparalleled since the Crusaders" (Elon). Joseph Stalin plotted against the Jews in his infamous doctors' plot (see Solzhenit-syn, p. 638) and, in spite of englightened public statements to the contrary, anti-Semitism still smolders hotly in the Soviet Union today.

Senator Henry Jackson has tried to influence more favorable emigration laws for Jews wishing to leave Russia. One of the strongest arguments he put forward were our financial dealings with Moscow. Time and again, the Senator urged a policy wherein America would continue economic favors to Russia, only if she in turn showed a relaxation of her restrictions against Jewish emigration.

Could it be that American bankers were making loans to Russia—which seemed less secure, less profitable than lending money at home—to aid Jews?

Are Rockefellers of Jewish Descent?

In 1960 a scholarly New Yorker named Malcolm H. Stern published a large book called *Americans of Jewish Descent*. It traced the history of 25,000 American Jews back into the eighteenth, seventeenth, and even sixteenth centuries. Stephen Birmingham says that certain people "bought a number of copies of the book and sent them to friends . . . including quite a few Christians whom in his researches, Dr. Stern had discovered to be of Jewish descent. To a few of the latter Dr. Stern's book must have come of something of a shock. Who would, for example, expect to find the Rockefellers in the book?" (*The Grandees*, pp. 1-3.)

If the Rockefeller family had descended from ancient Jewish nobility, as Stephen Birmingham's book suggested, it would not be difficult to explain the fact that they were Christian, according to the author. He spoke of the many who through the years accepted the Christian faith, such as Benjamin Disraeli, prime minister of England, and close friend of the Rothschilds.

One thing that true Christians and Jews had in common

was a profound respect for the Old Testament prophets, like Isaiah and Daniel. In the Rockefeller Church at Pocantico Hills, among the windows on which carefully selected scriptures were written, was the Scripture telling of the angel who appeared to Daniel to promise him wisdom and understanding for the last days.

Russia's Great Mistake

Prophets of the Bible not only declared in scores of passages that Israel would return to the homeland, they also spoke of a day when Russia, with her allies, would invade Israel. The prophet Ezekiel, in 587 B.C., described Russia's invasion of the Middle East. In 38:18 he says that "Gog [Russia] shall come against the land of Israel." Russia threatened such an invasion in the fall of 1973, but President Nixon ordered a world-wide alert of American armed forces with a command to make ready atomic weapons. Russia did not move further, but the danger was there.

President Ford calls the war peril in the Middle East "very serious." Secretary of State Henry Kissinger, in an interview with *Business Week* magazine, said that he "refused to rule out the use of force in the Middle East" (*Los Angeles Times*, January 13, 1975).

This area is certainly the most strategic point for deciding the contest between the super powers. The Suez Canal has often been referred to by historians as "the jugular vein of the world." Add to that the fact that, with the food crisis of the world related to the availability of fertilizer, the fantastic deposits of the Dead Sea are of growing significance.

Then, last but not least, of course, are the Mid-East oil fields. The prophet Ezekiel describes most dramatically Russia making a quick move to capture the prizes mentioned: "thou shalt think an evil thought: And thou shalt say, I will go . . . to take a spoil . . ." (38:10-12). And the prophet repeatedly states that "it shall be in the latter days" (38:16).

A friend once told me of a film from the Pentagon which he was privileged to see. It had been taken by Russian photographers during one of their giant military maneuvers. My friend said it was one of the most awesome sights he had ever seen. From an elevated position the cameraman apparently swung the camera on a complete 360-degree circle, photographing military maneuvers on both land and in the air.

"Honestly," he said, "it was breathtaking. As far as the eye could see in all directions, there were tanks on the ground and planes in the air. They resembled a great storm cloud."

Could this have been what the prophet saw in his vision when he wrote, "Thou shalt ascend and come like a storm, thou shalt be like a cloud to cover the land, thou, and all thy bands, and many people with thee" (38:9)? This will be the moment when all history hangs in the balance. But Ezekiel declares that God Himself will act with sudden judgment, "It shall come to pass at the same time when Gog shall come against the land of Israel, saith the Lord GOD, that my fury shall come up in my face. . . . And I will rain upon him, and upon his bands, and upon the many people that are with him, an overflowing rain, and great hailstones, fire and brimstone" (38:18, 22).

In this great judgment Russia is destined to see in the near future five-sixths of her military might destroyed (Ezek. 39:2). The devastation will be beyond our comprehension, for "seven months shall the house of Israel be burying them" (Ezek. 39:12).

Sudden Destruction

A rattle of teacups caused me to glance at the doorway and see Verna in the entrance with a loaded tray.

"Don't you think it is time for a break?" she asked cheerily. "How about a cup of tea?"

"Great idea," I said, taking the tray from her. "Let's have it in the other room."

"How is the book progressing?" asked Verna, when we had finished our tea.

"Just before our break, I was engrossed in the study of the writings of Ezekiel, who wrote in 587 B.C. He declared in the latter days that Russia and her allies would march into the Middle East and be destroyed.

"He told of fire coming from heaven, and destroying five-sixths of the Russian army. The prophet says it will take seven years to cleanse the land. Some atomic scientists talk about seven years being required to clear an area of radiation. The prophet also speaks of seven months being required to bury the dead. This might also be because of atomic radiation hazards. One thing is certain, it will be a time of terrible destruction.

"The other day, Professor O.G. Villard, Jr., who incidentally received the Meritorious Civilian Service Award, the highest honor the U.S. AirForce presents to civilians, said that the 'Next world war will be over in days' (*San Jose Mercury*, January 16, 1976).

"You know, Verna," I said thoughtfully, "many interpreted the withdrawal of America from Vietnam as weakness. However, this could be very misleading to some of America's critics."

"Why do you say that?"

"Because the seeming defeat was based on a limited use of military weapons. Billions of dollars are being spent today on super weapons that have never been used. There is a difference between weakness and restraint. Thus far there had been a restraint in using the major weapons. But what would happen if survival was at stake? Besides, only recently, Henry Kissinger pledged that the U.S. will never abandon Israel" (*International Herald Tribune*, April 6, 1976).

"Supposing Russia and her allies made a sudden move into the Middle East, and America did not come to her defense," Verna asked seriously.

"Israel still has atomic weapons of her own and, even more important, *God.* In his book on Israel, Homer Duncan quotes Moshe Dayan as saying; 'Even if there are three against 100, or one against 50, there is a way to win' (*Israel*, p. 49). Duncan tells of Aluf Shlomo, chief chaplain of the Israeli army, drawing up a prayer that the Israeli soldiers could recite before they went to battle. That prayer included the words of Moses, 'When thou goest out to battle against thine enemies and seest . . . a people more than thou, be not afraid of them. . . . For the LORD your God is he that goeth with you, to fight for you against your enemies, to save you' (Deut. 20:1, 4).

"Old Testament history records that the Israelites were often outnumbered on the battlefield. Gideon challenged hordes of Midianites which were 'as the sand by the seaside for multitude' (Judg. 7:12) with a mere three hundred men. Saul was outnumbered by the Philistines, as was Hezekiah by the Assyrians. But in each of these cases—and in dozens more like them—God intervened according to His promise in Deuteronomy. As Jonathan, the prince of Israel, rejoiced, 'The Lord hath delivered them into our hands' (I Sam. 14:10).

"Do you remember the six day war fought in 1967, how Israel was so vastly outnumbered? Before that battle, some Israelis quoted the words of Zechariah, 'In that day shall the LORD defend the inhabitants of Jerusalem; and he that is feeble among them at that day shall be as David; and the house of David shall be as God . . .' (12:8). So, even if the Russian forces invading Israel in the future are vastly superior, 'God will destroy the nations that come against Jerusalem' (Zech. 12:9).

As we sat in silence, absorbed with these truths, I thought of the comment concerning Russia that Mr. Teng made to President Ford, when he said: "Today it is the country which most vehemently preaches peace that is the most dangerous source of war. Rhetoric about detente cannot cover the stark reality of the growing danger of war. The wind is blowing harder and harder and nothing can prevent the storm" (*U.S. News and World Report*, p. 14, December 15, 1975).

I found myself repeating once more the words of Lenin: "We have not forgotten that war will return. While Capitalism and Socialism live side by side, they cannot live in peace: One or the other will ultimately triumph" (*On Peaceful Coexistence*, p. 68).

"Yes," I said, "Lenin meant exactly what he said, that 'peaceful coexistence is an agreement concerning war' (*Ibid.*). And his followers today apparently agree, even as Soviet Defense Minister Andrei Grechko declares: 'Detente must never be interpreted as the slackening of the ideological war, which must go on so long as Capitalism exists' (*Oregonian*, June 6, 1974).

Can Capitalism Survive?

"And," added Verna thoughtfully, "if Russia should march with force into the Middle East, and suffer a defeat from which she would not soon recover, would this mean that the bankers of the West would be the money masters of the world?"

"Only for a few months," I replied. "If the Bible is true, Capitalism will also come under the control of a world leader, who is called in the Bible the prince of the world."

Verna at this point started for the kitchen with the tray of empty tea cups, saying, "What a drama! What a day!"

"And," I added, "what a climax!"

Chapter 6
Father To Son

The sound of a car horn from the street below caused me to step to the window.

"Would you believe it?" I exclaimed enthusiastically "It's Lee and Paul."

Moments later our sons entered the room with greetings and embraces.

"Why didn't you tell us you were driving up from Southern France?" asked Verna.

"We wanted to surprise you," they replied.

Late that evening when Paul decided it was bedtime, and Verna, too, agreed that she was feeling sufficiently weary to say goodnight, Lee, our older son, showed little interest in sleep, and wanted to stay up longer and talk.

"How is your book progressing, dad?" he asked. "You told me some time ago that the title would be *The Money Master of the World.* Are you telling your readers who the money master is?"

"I haven't reached that point yet."

"Do you mind telling me what you have written?"

"Not at all. To date I have put on paper what I feel to be important questions of the day, and answers to which may be found by looking at the history of finance, and the future predictions of the prophets. The Bible speaks of a day when 'men's hearts would fail them for fear' (Luke 21:26). Many doctors and psychologists feel that concern for the financial future is a real source of illness. Old people fear that the value of dollars is being destroyed by inflation. The young fear a faltering economy that cannot assure them of employment."

"That's true in France," said Lee. "The other day the press declared that 500,000 young people under twenty-five years were unemployed. In Paris, there have been 25,000 students on strike for a week, and students have been marching in another thirty French cities" (*International Herald Tribune*, April 16, 1976).

"Fear," I continued, "seems to touch every class. The housewives see the computer codes being placed on packages of food, and fear future rationing. The businessman sees thousands of small businesses being swallowed up by the big combines, and wonder how long they can survive independently. Landowners fear that new legislation may affect the use of land. Hoarders of gold express concern that the price of that metal might drop. Others fear that there could be a repetition of 1934 when the government asked for all the gold.

"Most of all, Lee, the average individual feels that he is too weak to compete with the big powers which seem to be gaining control of the masses. And, speaking of power, I have been interested in reviewing the struggles of the centuries between government leaders and financiers. This power struggle is as old as history.

"Writers like Kenan say Louis McFadden declared that founders of the Federal Reserve System favored a world government including Russia. If this be true, we ask if they would favor a world under Marx, Lenin, Stalin, or the present Soviet KGB? If not, what kind of a world government would they desire, and why?

"I remind the readers that not all one worlders are Communists like Marx. Fuller would favor a world government in order to pool the world resources and feed the hungry. Pope Paul would favor a world body like the U.N. that could spare man the destruction of war. Some bankers present logical reasons for desiring a world system that would support world trade."

"But," asked Lee, "if Russia is building her military strength in a bid for world control, can the power of the Western bankers match such might?"

"In the book, Lee, we refer to the history of money power. We mention that the banking brains of the West might well have a strategy that could support the U.N. with the International Monetary Fund being the center of future banking."

"Interesting," replied Lee. "Very interesting."

"Especially," I replied, "when you stop and think that the IMF was actually born in 1944 and the U.N. in 1945. Today with suggestions being made that world travel accounts and the billions from oil profits be handled through the IMF, this could be a key to world control."

For a moment, Lee sat in silence, looking off into space, and when he spoke it was as though speaking to himself, "It is like a tremendous drama, isn't it?"

World Control: The Prize

"True," I replied. "It's like a chess game being played by champions for the prize, world control."

"And what if Russia sees herself losing?"

"Then," I replied, "in the views of men like Solzhenitsyn, she will resort to military strength."

"Didn't Lenin talk about detente being a period of economic war?"

"Yes, he did, and predicted war would return. And I would say in the present contest, the Russian bankers do not have a background of brilliance and ingenuity to compare with those of the West."

"But," added Lee, "she may feel superior in military might."

"Probably, and decide this is the best way for her to achieve her victory. She may gamble on moving with massive strength into the Middle East."

"Do you believe this will result in an atomic war?"

"Lee," I replied, "this was the very question under consideration when you and Paul arrived today. You know for years I have been a student of Bible prophecy, and I believe the prophets are the only ones who can answer this question."

"Many today talk about Armageddon."

"True, and this well may be the commencement."

'Do the prophets declare the winner?"

"Yes, they tell of God in fury defending Israel in a battle that results in five-sixths of the Russian forces being destroyed."

"Then this would result in a victory for capitalism and the West?"

"For a brief period, yes."

"Why do you say for a brief period?"

"Because the prophets declare that following this battle, men will form a world government. To protect themselves from further destruction, they will be ready to place the arms of the world under the control of a single committee."

"But this is not a new thought."

"No, Jack Kennedy long ago wrote Article 7277, suggesting that something of this nature be done in the interest of preserving peace. I believe the article was entitled Freedom from War. Somewhere back in America I have a copy of this in my files. Some said, even in Kennedy's day, that it would probably take another atomic bomb to make men willing to accept world government. Naturally men are afraid of atomic warfare, but they are also afraid of a world system which could place a leader in control of such power.

"One with control of an atomic arsenal would surely have power unparalleled. Incidentally, Lee, when in Brussels some years ago, I talked with Dave Oliver who had been twenty-eight years with the Atomic Energy Commission. Dave reminded us that President Truman wielded the power that released the first atomic bomb on Japan. When I left Dave that night, I read in the Bible concerning a coming world ruler who would make fire come down from heaven and to whom power was given over all kindreds and tongues and nations (Rev. 13:13, 7).

"I wonder," I said, "if possibly Harold Urey might have been familiar with these Bible prophecies? His name is synonymous with the A-bomb.

(Professor Urey of University of Chicago wrote 'Regarding giving the secre.s of atomic power to a World Government, such a super World Government is not a solution to world power. For there is the possibility that a tyrant will get control of the world through this instrument of atomic energy. The atomic bomb is characteristic of a tyrant's weapon. It is just the weapon that would enable a dictator to sit firmly in his seat and no one could do anything about it" (Taken from *You Can Know the Future*, by Wilbur M. Smith, p. 59).

A World President

"Before you arrived, Lee," I continued, "I was reviewing the preliminary draft of a World Constitution described in Britannica Encyclopedia's *Great Ideas Today*, *1971*. On page 345, I studied the chart showing the proposed structure for this world government. It would include a chamber of guardians, a supreme court, a grand council, a tribune of the people, and a president.

"Imagine, Lee," a president of the world! What power that person would possess! If a world government was formed as described by those who drafted this constitution, the president would have what no other man in history possessed: world control!"

"And you believe that such is coming?" asked my son seriously.

"The prophets in the Bible declare there will be a man who will rule the world for a brief period, and he not only will receive power from the people, the Bible declares he also will receive power from Satan.

"When I was your age, Lee, many ridiculed the thought that Satan existed. I recall a man being tried for murder. When asked by the judge why he committed the crime, he replied, 'The devil appeared unto me and instructed me to do it!' Angrily the judge shouted, 'Put him in a mental institution. No one but a crazy man believes in a devil!'

"Today, in contrast, the vast majority declare their belief in a devil. When Merv Griffin interviewed the producers of the film *The Exorcist*, the answers they gave to his questions were amazing."

"You heard them?"

"Yes," I replied. "For almost an hour they discussed the story of the film, its production, etc. But the most important comment came from the reporters who interviewed the people attending the movie. They asked them whether they did or did not believe in the existence of the devil. The answer was invariably yes!"

"Seriously?"

"They said almost without any exceptions the answer was in the affirmative."

"And the majority of those attending the movie, I understand, were young people?"

"Correct. When your mother was raised in Philadelphia, there was nothing like witchcraft taught in the schools. Today Lucy Garreston at Temple University in Philadelphia teaches witchcraft in what is supposed to be a course in anthropology. I understand that the course is very popular. Other teachers are saying that the study of witchcraft is the 'in' thing today. Professor David Lindberg at the University of Wisconsin is quoted as saying that most of the young people of the next generation will believe in spell-casting witches. In Fordham University in New York, a course called 'devilology' is devoted to serious study of the devil. It deals with witchcraft, devil worship and demon lore.

"And it is not only in America. It is all over Europe and Britain also. For example, the last time we were in Brussels and Vienna, the film *The Exorcist*, was drawing much attention. One of the members of the British House of Commons went so far as to state that presently in Britain one in every five children was connected with witchcraft."

"Speaking of witches," said Lee. "Didn't Hunt of the Watergate crowd write a book called *The Coven?*"

"Right. Perhaps he bewitched the rest," I chuckled. "Seriously, Lee, isn't it amazing the fantastic reception that William Peter Blatty's book *The Exorcist* has received? But the reception is rather easily explained. Thirty years ago, a book as bad as this would have collected dust on the shelf. Apart from a rather colorful opening chapter, the rest of the book is filthy and phony. The language used by the mother of the child would suggest that she, perhaps as much as her twelve-year-old daughter, was possessed."

"And this is the story that is a best seller, and the movie that millions line up to see in theaters?"

"Right, and as I said, there is a reason. The popularity of

MONEY MASTER OF THE WORLD

both the book and the film pertain greatly to the time of their release. The story was not responsible for making the readers or viewers believers in the devil. The film and book were accepted by a generation that had already returned to belief in Satan and demons. I could not help but note some of the phrases that appeared in the world's papers concerning Blatty's book.

"The New York Times Book Review: '. . . it comes to grips with the forces of evil incarnate.'

"Los Angeles Magazine: 'overflows with intelligence and insight.'

"The Sunday Express (London): '. . . the battle between the priest and the demon. He wonders if he still believes in God. But God or not, he swiftly comes to believe in the devil.'

"St. Louis Post-Dispatch: '. . . shake the complacency of believer and non-believer alike.'

"Abilene Reporter-News: '. . . it touches on things in this world that cannot be explained away rationally.' "

"Incidentally," said Lee, "does Blatty quote from the Bible?"

"Yes, he does, in the very introduction. He quotes Luke 8:27-30, 'Now when Jesus stepped ashore, there met him a certain man who for a long time was possessed by a devil. Many times it had laid hold of him and he was bound with chains . . . but he would break the bonds asunder . . . and Jesus asked him saying, "What is thy name?" and he said, "Legion". . . .' "

"Would you say that Blatty's book is in general agreement with the Bible?"

"In acknowledging the devil? Yes, but apart from that fact, I'd say *no!*"

"Why?"

"Well, in the first place, look at the two pitiful exorcists, old Father Merin dies by the bedside of the devil-possessed girl, and the other priest, Father Karras, in the climax of the story jumps out of the window to his death with the devil in him. This is a far cry from the report Christ's disciples gave when they returned from the missionary journey on which He sent them. They returned 'with joy, saying, Lord, even the devils are subject unto us through thy name' (Luke 10:17).

"And speaking of the contrast between Blatty's book and the Bible, you have often heard the statement that 'nothing is as deceiving as half-truth.' Well, the only glimpse that Blatty gives of the devil and his work is the portrayal of a young girl wallowing in her filth in her private room. This might be one example, but the Bible also shows Satan deceiving men and nations with subtlety, and Paul says: 'And no marvel; for Satan himself is transformed into an angel of light' (2 Cor. 11:14).

"Christ occasionally referred to Satan as the prince of this world. In John 14:30 he described him by that title. And, when the devil came to tempt Jesus in the wilderness, he made an amazing claim. Regarding the kingdoms of this world, he said: 'All this power will I give thee, and the glory of them: for it was delivered unto me; and to whomsoever I will I give it' (Luke 4:5, 6).

"Christ did not contest Satan's claim. It seems evident that once in the distant past the glories of this planet were somehow placed under Satan's jurisdiction.

"Ezekiel tells us of the origin of the devil. He was apparently one of God's superlative creations, an anointed cherub of great authority who was virtually perfect, until iniquity was one day discovered in him. His heart, the prophet explains, was lifted up because of his beauty and he corrupted his wisdom by reason of his brightness" (Ezek. 28:13-17).

"Dad, doesn't Isaiah speak of him too?"

"Yes, Lee, he called him 'the son of the morning' and

explains that he fell because he aspired to be like God—to usurp God's place.

"Satan wanted to be worshiped as Christ was worshiped. And he has never lost that desire. He told Christ he would give him all the glories of earth if He would only worship him. Lucifer apparently had sufficient influence to persuade a third of the angels to follow him in his rebellion. This warfare in the heavens must have been something surpassing man's imagination. John says simply: 'There was war in heaven: Michael and his angels fought against the dragon; and the dragon fought and his angels, and prevailed not; neither was their place found any more in heaven. And the great dragon was cast out, that old serpent, called the Devil, and Satan, which deceiveth the whole world: he was cast out into the earth, and his angels were cast out with him' (Rev. 12:7-9).

Two Wars

"Lee," I asked, "what are the main things you would want to know about any war?"

"I would want to know, first, who was fighting, and then why they were fighting, and how they fought, and, of course, how did the war end?"

"Then would it not be reasonable to suppose that the same four questions would apply equally to spiritual warfare?"

"I would say so, dad. Why?"

"If Lucifer leads his angels against God because of his desire to be worshiped like Christ, we should consider his strategy. St. John tells how Satan will seek world control at the close of this age, and force mankind to worship as he commands.

"Lee, I was just about your age when Hitler was ascending to power. Germany, like the rest of Europe and America, had felt the pain of depression, and was ripe for a dictatorial savior. Do you remember my telling you about Karl Fix. He worked in the German Intelligence Department in Berlin and knew Hitler well."

"Didn't you work with Mr. Fix for a number of years, dad?"

"True. I met him after the war, and at the time of our acquaintance he was a devout Christian, in total contrast to the Nazis."

"Did he ever talk about Hitler?"

"Only on a very few occasions."

"Did he ever discuss the plot to kill Hitler?"

"Yes, on one occasion when we were alone in Berlin, standing by the monument that had been erected to the leaders who were executed for their attempt on Hitler's life. Karl seemed visibly moved by painful memories of the past. Undoubtedly he had prayed a thousand times to forget. I asked myself sincerely if I should ask him to tell more about Hitler from his own personal observations. I was curious to know if he, like many other prominent men, thought that Hitler was possessed of a devil.

"Late on this particular day, we were just a few yards from the Russian sector. The old Reichstag building in the distance still stood black and ugly as it had the morning after it had been gutted by flames. It was here that our conversation turned naturally to the incident that took place on July 20, 1944, in Adolf Hitler's conference hut at Rastenburg. Karl began to review that memorable event in a low voice, as though talking to himself more than to me.

" 'Count Claus Stauffenberg entered the conference room to join Hitler and the other officers,' he said. 'In his hand he carried a leather briefcase, in which he had placed a two-pound bomb. Moments before, he had opened the briefcase secretly in an adjoining room and had broken the bomb's glass capsule containing acid which would dissolve the insulation on a thin wire in ten minute's time and explode the bomb. After placing the briefcase with the bomb under the table near the feet of Hitler, he turned to Field Marshal Wilhelm Keitel and whispered, "I've got an urgent phone call to make; I'll be back in a minute."

" 'As Colonel Heinz Brandt moved his chair closer to the table to get a better view of a military map, his feet touched Stauffenberg's briefcase on the floor. Reaching down he picked up the case and set it in another location farther from Hitler. By doing this, he unknowingly spared Hitler from a certain death. Moments later a deafening roar echoed and black clouds of smoke poured from the building. Four men were killed and twenty wounded in the explosion. Hitler, partly protected by the heavy table, escaped death but was partially paralyzed in one arm.

" 'For several hours, following the explosion, confusion reigned among the men who had thus plotted to seize the government. In Berlin, General Friedrich Olbricht was to give the signal Operation Valkyrie.'

"Why," I asked Karl, "did they choose the name valkyrie?"

" 'Valkyries,' he said, 'were, according to the old Norse legends, female emissaries of Odin, the king of the gods. In time of battle, valkyries might appear either as beautiful women in shining armour, or as gigantic hags weaving patterns with dismembered bodies and human skulls.'

"Karl's blue eyes teared ever so slightly as he turned his gaze from me as though looking down the corridors of the past. 'I should have been with those who died,' he said softly, as though speaking more to himself than to me. 'It was only a miracle of divine providence that spared me.'

"Later on I appreciated more than ever the significance of his remark, when I learned the scope of Hitler's retaliation against those who were implicated in the July 20th plot. C.L. Sulzberger, in his *American Heritage History of World War*

II, said that of the almost fifteen thousand suspects who were arrested, about five thousand were put to death. 'Some of the more distinguished plotters were tried in a specially constituted 'people's court,' humiliated, and then slowly strangled on meathooks. They were filmed in their agony on Hitler's order and the film was then shown to selected military audiences as a warning.'

"Would you say that Hitler and Himmler and the like were demon possessed?" asked my son.

"Felix Kersten, the Nazi doctor, said the actions of Hitler and Himmler transcended the human and entered into another world. But Trevor Ravenscroft has written an especially intriguing book."

"Tell me more."

"Ravenscroft was born in England in 1921. He served as a commando officer during World War II and was captured in an attempt to assassinate Rommel in Africa. As a prisoner of war from 1941 to 1945, he actually escaped three times, but was recaptured on each occasion. After the war he became a journalist until he left that position to lecture in history at London and Edinburgh. But my particular interest in Trevor Ravenscroft is in his association for twelve years with Dr. Walter Johannes Stein. If any man knew Hitler, his early life, his rise to power, his ambitions and accomplishments, it was Stein."

My son nodded for me to continue.

"Stein," I said, "was born in Vienna in 1891, the son of a wealthy Austrian barrister. Although he graduated in science from Vienna, he wrote his doctoral dissertation in philosophy. Stein's reputation reached far beyond his native Austria. He lectured in the palace of Kemal Ataturk of Turkey, and established his academic influence in Germany through his extensive work in medieval history. Stein escaped to Britain to avoid arrest by the Nazis in 1933. Actually it wasn't so much that they wanted to imprison him, instead they wanted him to serve in the SS occult bureau. He was, perhaps, one of the leading experts on the dark sciences in Germany.

"Ravenscroft wanted to know more about Nazi occultism, and so made it a point to become acquainted with Dr. Stein. After twelve years of study under this brilliant man, he wrote *The Spear of Destiny*.

"Pardon me a moment," I said, as I moved toward the study. "I'll get his book and let you hear a few quotes on this remarkable subject."

Returning with Ravenscroft's book, Lee and I continued our conversation on Hitler.

"Early in youth Hitler experimented with drugs, 'Hitler assessed that the drugs could provide his most direct short cut to transcendent consciousness' (p. 80). Hitler aspired to Luciferic possession, 'The drug-induced awareness now channeled into his consciousness served to guide him toward his sinister and inhuman goals of personal power, tyranny and world conquest' (p. 81). Stein spoke of the demoniac spirit which overshadowed Hitler, who said, in a press interview, 'I move like a sleep walker where providence dictates' (p. 65).

"Ravenscroft observed, '. . . it was as though Hitler himself was listening to the extraneous intelligence which had temporarily taken over his soul.' And he quoted August Kubizek, 'In moments of greatest excitement it was as if another being spoke out of his body and moved him as much as it did me' (p. 3).

"And Dr. Stein, 'His whole physiognomy and stance appeared transformed as if some mighty spirit now inhabited his very soul creating within and around him a kind of evil transfiguration' (p. 64).

"At one time Hitler told Rauschning: 'The Superman is

living among us now! He is here . . . I have seen the New Man. He is intrepid and cruel. I was afraid of him' (Hermann Rauschning, *Hitler Speaks*).

"I believe much the same could be said about Himmler," I added. "When the first allied army units arrived at Buchenwald concentration camp, near the old cultural center of Weimar, they stood dumbfounded before a spectacle of unspeakable horror. Piles of false teeth, bales of women's hair, and hundreds of pairs of baby shoes were all neatly piled near the skeleton-like bodies waiting cremation.

"Himmler would excoriate Goering for shooting a deer in the woods, but would stand unmoved when camp guards would lash helpless women strapped to punishment racks or when trainloads of men and women and children entered the gas chambers to die gruesomely.

"Our men took Himmler prisoner at Bremer-Vorde and brought him to interrogation camp 031. He had tried to disguise himself by removing his pince-nez, placing a black patch over his eye and shaving off his moustache. In spite of this he was quickly recognized, but before they could ask him any questions, he bit a small vial of cyanide hidden in his mouth and, fifteen minutes later, he was dead. Before he drew his final breath, two death masks were made of his face. Those who studied them stared in amazement at what they saw. One mask seemed peaceful and normal and the other was so hideous and cruel, it resembled the face of a devil more than a man.

"Dr. Felix Kersten, Himmler's physiotherapist, said, 'There was a dichotomy in his nature. He was like two people; one was the personality of an ordinary schoolteacher or clerk. The other entered into realms which transcended the human and entered into another world.'

"The horrors of Naziism certainly caused many to return to belief in devils. In the introduction to *The Exorcist* three words sit across the bottom of the page: *Dachau, Auschwitz, Buchenwald.*"

"In other words," replied Lee, "he points to these Nazi horror camps as visible evidences of satanic work?"

Why Did Hitler Try to Destroy the Jews?

I had become so engrossed in the weight of the subject, I scarcely heard Lee's question. The things I was saying seemed too extreme to be real. "Excuse me," I said, "yes, I think that's a correct deduction."

"You have been to Dachau?"

"Yes, Lee," I replied. "I have been to Dachau."

"How would you describe it?"

"Lee," I answered sadly, "one cannot. Amos Elon wrote: 'Language limps, it invariably breaks down under the weight of the subject. The loudest cries are the mute ones. The Jews were singled for destruction not because of what they did or refrained from doing, not because of faith or politics, but simply because they were there.'

"It doesn't seem real, does it, that this could happen in the twentieth century?"

"No," I replied. "Alsop said that '. . . for reasons one cannot exactly understand, the historical process in the twentieth century has become more cruel, more bloodstained, and more dangerous than it ever was in the simpler past" (*Oregonian* June 28, 1974).

"Dad, I've heard you mention a doctor's plot during Stalin's regime that was utterly diabolical but which never materialized."

"Right, Solzhenitsyn says it is one plan of Stalin that failed."

"Can you tell me more about it?"

"It seems that an elderly woman named Dr. Timasuk, an electrocardiograph specialist, supposedly told Stalin that she had discovered some Jewish doctors who were plotting against certain Soviet leaders. These doctors were to be convicted, condemned, and hanged publicly in Red Square. Trained agitators would thereupon arouse the public to the point of rushing into an anti-Jewish pogrom.

"And here Stalin was to pretend to save the Jewish people from the mobs by shipping them off in the night to a place of safety. But that place of safety, according to Solzhenitsyn, was to be in the barracks which had been especially built for them in Siberia."

For a moment there was silence, and then Lee asked, "Do you think that Jewish doctors really plotted against Stalin, or his leaders?"

"Not according to Nikita Khrushchev. At the twentieth party congress he said, 'When we examined the case after the death of Stalin, we found it to be fabricated from beginning to end' (H. Montgomery Hyde, *Stalin*, pp. 558, 559).

Again neither of us spoke for a moment.

Finally Lee asked, "But why would Hitler and Stalin try to destroy the Jews?"

"Maybe," I replied, "it was as Amos Elon said, 'because they were there.' "

"But," persisted Lee, "there has to be a deeper reason."

'And there is," I answered.

"Can you tell me?"

"If you want to sit and talk a little longer, for the answer is not simple."

"It's more important to me than another half hour of sleep."

'Well enough, let's begin by quoting Stalin himself, who said in the presence of Churchill and Roosevelt, 'Satan is my Ally' (Hyde, p. 495). If Satan was his ally, we may understand why he and his successors would like to destroy Israel.

"You recall that I explained Satan's origin in heaven as the anointed cherub who aspired to take God's place. In his rebellion he and his angels were driven from heaven and cast down to earth. We saw, too, when he told Jesus that he, Satan, had jurisdiction over the earth and its kingdoms, Jesus did not dispute it. In fact, Jesus, on another occasion, actually referred to him as the prince of this world. But Christ did not bow down to Satan nor worship him, for He knew the time was coming when Satan's jurisdiction over earth would end. The devil also was aware of this. Matthew tells of the demoniacs whose demons complained to Jesus, 'Art thou come hither to torment us before the time?' (8:29).

And John declares that, at the close of this age, the devil will have great wrath 'because he knoweth that he hath but a short time' (Rev.12:12).

Satan knew that God intended to break his diabolical grasp on this planet and to establish on earth a kingdom of righteousness and peace. Satan also knew that God, long ago, had revealed unto Abraham that the Jewish race would fill an important place in the establishment of this kingdom which would bring lasting blessing to all mankind. The angel, Gabriel, who spoke with Daniel, said he had come to give him skill and understanding. Gabriel told him of the day when God would use his people to 'bring in everlasting righteousness' (Dan. 9:24). And the apostle Paul spoke of his brethren 'who are Israelites; to whom pertaineth the adoption, and the glory, and the covenants, and the giving of the law, and the service of God, and the promise' (Rom. 9:4).

"Satan not only knew what the prophets said, he also knew what men like Tolstoy, called king of Russian literature, wrote:

The Jew is that sacred being who has brought down from Heaven the Everlasting Fire, and has enlightened with it the entire world. He is the religious source, spring, and fountain out of which all the rest of the peoples have drawn their beliefs and their religions. The Jew is the emblem of eternity. He whom neither slaughter nor torture of himself for years could destroy; he whom neither fire nor sword, nor inquisition was able to wipe from the face of the earth; he who was the first to produce the oracles of God; he who has been for so long a time the guardian of prophecy, and who has transmitted it to the rest of the world . . . such a nation cannot be destroyed, the Jew is as everlasting as eternity itself (Anton Darms, *The Jew Returns to Israel*).

"As a small boy, Lee, I am sure that you remember learning the verses written by Isaiah:

'For unto us a child is born, unto us a son is given; and the government shall be upon his shoulder and his name shall be called, Wonderful, Counsellor, The Mighty God, The Everlasting Father, The Prince of Peace. Of the increase of his government and peace there shall be no end, upon the throne of David, and upon his kingdom, to order it and establish it with judgment and with justice from henceforth even forever (9:6, 7).' "

"So," said Lee, "because Satan knows these prophecies and sees the Jews, chosen of God, as an obstacle in his drive for world government, he has tried through the centuries to destroy them?"

"That is right. He has worked through men like Torquemada, Diego Deza of the Inquisition, Hitler, and Stalin."

"Do you think it could happen again?"

"Yes."

"And again and again?" asked my son sadly.

"No, Lee, not again and again. God has declared through the prophets that there will be a final time known as Jacob's trouble, but this will be the last, and will usher in the golden reign of peace."

"If God is strong enough to eventually terminate Satan's influence on earth, why has He delayed judgment so long?"

"That, Lee, is a question as old as the ages. If we knew all of the answers, we would be God."

"But is there no answer?"

"God's ways are not man's ways, Lee. Man writes laws intended to bring swift punishment to the guilty, but God's patience with this rebellious planet seems to know no bounds. When God created this planet, he had an audience, and Job says that audience was so impressed that 'all the sons of God shouted for joy' " (38:7).

I venture to say that this audience which rejoiced at the wonders of creation may have shuddered at Satan's rebellion. And God in His justice has allowed the centuries to pass to prove the awfulness of that sin in its full result.

"Before the age of peace can finally come, two things must happen. First, the power and influence of Satan must be broken "

"And the second?" asked Lee.

"Man has to reach the place where he sees that he cannot govern this world without God. Both of these tremendous points seem to be drawing closer."

"You have been a student of prophecy for a long time, dad."

"Most of my life."

"Does it ever disturb you when some suggest conflicting things under the name of prophecy?"

"Not too much. Most of the conflict is imagined and what is not can be resolved if you follow the rules. When men follow the rules of study, and this is essential, then they speak the same thing.

"I have enjoyed talking with you and appreciate your desire to enquire concerning these truths. It seems today there are three kinds of people: one that does not want to enquire, another that looks at the future without faith and is filled with fear, and another that views all of these fearful things with the light of the prophets and has faith that God's day will dawn.

"We could talk all night," I said, standing to my feet. "But I think you should get a little sleep before you leave for France. I don't want you to fall asleep at the wheel. When you come the next time, we'll talk more about these things."

As we walked toward the bedrooms, my son asked, "Incidentally, dad, why have you chosen the title, *The Money Master of the World*, for your new book?"

"Because," I answered, "in Satan's final bid for world control, money will play a very important part."

Later before I turned out the lights, I glanced into my son's room and saw that he was already asleep. But I saw something else that filled me with joy. It was the expression of peace upon his face.

"Only three classes of people," I repeated as I turned away. "Those who won't face the issues of the day with honesty, those who study the world situation without faith and are filled with fear, and those who view the entire spectrum in the light of the Bible, and have peace."

As I reached for the light switch, I recalled Jesus' promise, "ye shall know the truth and the truth shall make you free" (John 8:32). How wonderful to be free from fear, and to be able to face a new day with faith.

Chapter 7

The Rulers of the Darkness of This World

From the balcony, Verna and I waved goodbye to the boys below, and watched our sons enter the car and disappear around the corner on their way back to France.

"It's always difficult to say goodbye to the boys, but we did have a good visit," said Verna, as she turned toward the kitchen.

"It was good," I replied as I entered the study.

Once in the study, I followed the usual custom of reading the Bible before looking at any other research material. I opened to the book of Ephesians, and read: "For we wrestle not against flesh and blood, but against principalities and powers, against the rulers of the darkness of this world, against spiritual wickedness in high places" (6:12).

In describing our warfare with Satan, John said, "He deceiveth the whole earth" (Rev. 12:9). Christ said, "He is a liar and the father of it" (John 8:44).

Ye Shall Be As Gods

When Satan first tempted man to follow him, he promised, "Ye shall be as gods" (Gen. 3:5).

Only a few years ago, many thought they could run the world without help from God. Within the halls of the U.N. I had heard men say, "If you give a man a fish you give him a meal, but if you teach him how to catch fish, you give him food for the rest of his life." Man felt that his technology could solve the problems of mankind, and that UNESCO, the educational arm of the U.N., could teach the whole world the answers to her needs. A speaker from the United Nations Agricultural Organization in Geneva said, "For the first time in the history of man it is possible for everybody to survive at a high standard of living" (Fuller, p. 123).

Some leaders such as Dr. Julian Huxley, the first Director General of the United Nations Educational Scientific Cultural Organization, not only inferred that God was no longer needed, he plainly declared Him to be unwanted. Dr. Huxley said, "There is a slight trace of God still brooding over our world like the smile of a cosmic Cheshire cat, but science and learning will soon rub it out." But science and learning soon proved inadequate to meet man's basic needs.

While space age technology could send men to the moon, a quarter of the world's population watched these feats with empty stomachs. Those of UNESCO who dreamed of world literacy became discouraged. The newspapers carried headlines reading, "Ten-Year-Old Program to End Illiteracy Fails UNESCO Admits" (*International Herald Tribune*, February 6, 1976). And *Time* magazine, in a lengthy article, painted a grim picture of world illiteracy. More than three quarters of the combined populations of India, China, and Nepal cannot read or write. Similar statistics are reported for Africa while about a third of the Latin American populations are still illiterate (*Time*, February 22, 1975).

Poverty in many cases had slowed the rate of learning, and even more alarming was the fact that the world population was predicted to double every thirty-five years.

Failure To Bring Balance

As if the gross problems of malnutrition and illiteracy were not enough, we are faced by enormous inequities in the amounts of money people are paid for their services. While men and women stood in lines at the employment bureaus, hoping for any type of work which would enable them to care for their families, they read newspaper articles by men like Bernard Siegel, who wrote: "There is definitely something out of kilter with our economy when baseball pitcher Jim (Catfish) Hunter can get himself a $3,700,000 contract because he may win 100 or 125 games in the next five years. What is he doing for humanity to deserve this kind of money?" (*Los Angeles Times*).

On a recent flight, I picked up a copy of *Mainliner* magazine, and saw the salaries of one group of athletes:

Wilt Chamberlain, San Diego..............$600,000
Nate Archibald, Kansas City-Omaha....$450,000
Kareem Abdul-Jabbar, Milwaukee.......$400,000
Ernie DiGregario, Buffalo $400,000

And of course, the classic example was Pele, the soccer player from Brazil, who drew a salary four times that of his nation's president.

With one quarter of the world's wage earners making fifty dollars a year, and half the world hungry, there are others like a lady from California who has seven Rolls-Royces, and two Bentleys. And while some labor all year, unable to afford a vacation, Liz Taylor is willing to see a number of passengers denied their places on the plane in order that she might take with her to Moscow a ton and a half of luggage (*Los Angeles Times*, February 15, 1975).

I was in Dallas when H.L. Hunt passed away. The *Dallas Morning News* devoted a full page to his memory. I could not help but note one particular sentence: "When Hunt gave up cigars, he declared that it wasn't for reasons of health, but because he figured he had wasted $300,000 of his time each year taking the wrappers off cigars and lighting them" (November 30, 1974).

Some people did not have enough money last year to buy Christmas presents for their own children. How did they feel when they read that Elvis Presley gave five luxury cars away as gifts and that they cost him about $70,000 (*Los Angeles Times*, January 17, 1976)?

And then there was the sheik of Abu Dhabi, who decided that he would like an extra home in England. When he bought the famous Buxted Ark, Sussex, a fifty-room edifice on 327 acres of land, for $575,000, he exclaimed, "That represented my revenue from oil for just fifty-one minutes." The sheik reputedly gives about two and a half million dollars annually to each of his twenty sub-sheiks for pocket money. One of the younger sheiks said he had thirty-five cars the last time he counted them (*Toronto Star*, November 9, 1974).

The Wrong Kind of Freedom

In the sixties, some decided God was dead. Others concluded that even if He did live, His laws could be ignored. Textbooks began to appear in classrooms, such as Richard Hettlinger's *Living With Sex*. The theme of the book, and especially its treatment of homosexuality and common law living, seemed to be best expressed in the chapter entitled "Doing What Comes Naturally." It didn't take long to realize that the new morality was but the old immorality.

As men and women followed this perverted teaching, writers like Stephen Roberts asked, "What is tearing the American family apart?" *Time* listed the increasing rate of divorce in America. In 1920, there was one divorce for every seven married. In 1940, there was a divorce for every six. In 1960, one out of four marriages ended in divorce. And in

1970, there was one divorce for every three marriages (February 11, 1966).

Under the name of freedom, even the very young were confronted with pornographic magazines filling newsstands of drug stores, bus depots, restaurants, supermarkets, etc. Publishers of *Playboy* magazine announced in full-page ads that fifteen million dollars would be spent on one month's issue of *Playboy*. Pornographic magazines were not confined only to America. Every month *Playboy* magazine reaches thirty million men in 156 countries and territories throughout the world. The company's gross income in 1974 was $204,268,366.

Peter put it aptly, "while they promise them liberty, they themselves are the servants of corruption" (2 Pet. 2:19). That corruption surfaces literally in the virtual epidemic of venereal disease in America today. Dr. Charles A. Hoffman expressed his concern over the increase in social diseases in a news article, ". . . the problem is enormous. Over three million people become infected every year. I urge every concerned citizen to get involved in the fight" (*Sunday Herald*, Bellingham, Washington, January 11, 1976). From Geneva, Switzerland, the World Health Organization of the United Nations stated: "Sexually-transmitted diseases . . . are nonetheless spreading at an alarming rate . . . for the world as a whole the rate of venereal disease among teenagers, aged 15 to 19, is increasing at twice the rate for the entire population" (*Los Angeles Times*, November 16, 1974).

Aside from sexual license, we see all around us today a strident lawlessness masquerading as liberty and freedom. Paul told Timothy that disobedience to parents would be a sign of the last days (2 Tim. 3:1, 2). Marx had disdained his father and despised any authority that challenged his own.

Stalin had tried to kill his father. Where God's laws are spurned and parental authority ignored, lawlessness and anarchy rise accordingly. Theft is no longer committed only by professional criminals. Harvey Burnstein, chairman of the security committee of the American Hotel Association, said, "I estimate that one out of three guests takes something and the losses could reach a half a billion dollars this year. Guests take everything that isn't nailed down: bedspreads, lamps, TV sets, ashtrays, crested towels, furniture, silverware and even wallpaper."

This disrespect for property seemed to be spreading over all of the Western world. The *Dallas Morning News* (January 21, 1973) reported that on an average day London has 150 burglaries, 85 car thefts, 91 frauds, and 34 violent assaults. Murders occurred every fifth day. Statistics from the continent were equally alarming. Gangs of vicious young criminals were giving police in Western Europe a new and frustrating problem. In Rome, crime involving teenagers increased 30% in 24 months. In France, the number of persons under 18 appearing in minors' courts nearly tripled in 15 years. In West Germany, one third of all arrests involved persons under 21.

Another evidence of the spirit of our age is the leniency of our law enforcement agencies. Senator McClellan pointed out that "the chance of being punished for a serious crime is less than one in twenty" (*U.S. News and World Report*).

Reaping Corruption

It is apparent to me that we, as a nation and as individuals, are faced with the consequences of the law of sowing and reaping. We have sowed rebellion in the guise of leniency and we have reaped strong rebellion. It is an invariable biblical principle.

One writer stated, under the headline "Common Market Fraud," that "John Nott, Minister of State for the Treasury, came in reply Thursday to questions about the reports that about $120,000,000 had disappeared from the budget funds of the European Common Market."

While the public in Europe was accusing the leaders of the Common Market of "fraud," the leaders in turn were blaming the small businessmen and farmers of the same sin. "Frauds by small farmers and businessmen alike have cost the European Common Market hundreds of millions of dollars" (*Los Angeles Times*, December 12, 1974). Fraud and corruption were words appearing more frequently both at home and abroad.

Men who have sought to be free from the authority of God and from His laws that pertain to the home and moral standards, are not becoming more liberated. Instead they are becoming servants—servants to corruption and fear.

A writer in *Time* magazine asks, "Will Democracy Survive?" Another article reads, "From Iceland to Bonn: Governments Toppling." Listing the problems that plague the governments of America, Britain, Canada, Australia, Denmark and Italy, the writer says, "Economic headaches are toppling governments across the world" (*Los Angeles Times*, May 11, 1974). In the words of Paul Greenberg, there's "chaos all 'round and no leaders."

Nation Against Nation

Almost two thousand years before Jan Christian Smuts wrote the charter for the United Nations, stating the intention "to live together in peace with one another as good neighbors," Christ described this day by asserting that "nation shall rise against nation" (Matt. 24:7).

A day in the U.N. would convince anyone that the words of Christ were more apt. Even within ideological ranks the animosity is tremendous. For example, a Chinese (Communist) editorial aimed against Soviet leaders in Moscow states: "The iniquitous revisionist renegade clique . . . . A

109

coterie of greedy, profit-grabbing exploiters," [guilty of:] "corruption, thievery and malpractices," [who] "squander the fruits of labor plundered from the Soviet people" (*Los Angeles Times*, December 13, 1974).

The present prospects of peace seemed doomed like the failures of the past. For centuries man sought in vain for peace. Woodrow Wilson had run on a platform aimed to keep America out of war. But American boys were among the ten million who fell in World War I. At the close of that conflict, the same president in 1919 called the League of Nations "the hope of the world," but it proved to be futile hope.

And in a mammoth rally in the Chicago Coliseum, held in the interest of peace, a banner read: "A Warless World by 1920." The well-meaning members of that peace rally learned, however, that it took more than words and banners to make their world "warless."

Prior to World War II, President Roosevelt told America, as had President Wilson, that none of her sons would fight on foreign soil, but millions fought abroad and hundreds of thousands never returned. In the same year that the U.N. was born, Douglas MacArthur said on September 2, 1945, "Military Alliances, Balance of Power, League of Nations, all in turn have failed."

More and more it seemed that men were beginning to recognize their shortcomings and failures. From the shelves of the study, I took the third volume of *The Earth and the Universe*. The list of the learned people who contributed to this work was impressive. There were ten from Yale, seven from Harvard, seven from Columbia, and many more from prestigious universities at home and abroad. From the last page of Volume 3, I read that "Less than a century ago, scientists felt confident that little remained for them to do but perfect more accurate systems of measurements. There seemed to be no process in nature that could not be described in terms of mechanical laws." But, they continued, "For all the tremendous insight that modern physics has provided in separate realms, it has also added to the enigma of man's existence."

In summing up all that is said in *The Earth and the Universe*, the author describes modern man as "handicapped by his inadequate conceptions—confined in his prison house of senses—tormented with uncertainty—beset by doubts."

Even Dr. Huxley, the first Director General of UNESCO, who had spoken so arrogantly concerning man's ability to rule the world without God, said, before leaving this life in 1975, "It seems like the genetic stupidity, physical weakness, and mental instability of man will prove too great a burden for progress to be achieved." On April 6, 1976, the *International Herald Tribune* carried on its front page a picture of Dr. Henry Kissinger, and a five-column article with a caption reading "History is a tale of efforts that have failed, of aspirations that were not realized."

The following day, the front page featured the face of Dr. Linus Pauling, winner of Nobel prizes for Chemistry in 1954, and peace in 1962. It quoted Pauling as saying that "The looming catastrophe might well result in a world war which could destroy civilization and might well be the end of the human race. Or it might take the form of mass starvation among a world population that has been doubling every 35 years. Civilization might also end because of the collapse of the systems upon which it depends."

Distress of Nations With Perplexity

Some who had entered the space age confident that they could build their utopian world without God were coming to the conclusion that their formulas were failing. The U.N. had not brought peace, modern agricultural technology was not feeding the hungry, the program of UNESCO was not achieving world literacy, and the New morality produced an epidemic of venereal disease.

Christ had declared that this age would end with "distress of nations with perplexity" (Luke 21:25). The *International Herald Tribune* (April 14, 1976) reported that "After Harassment by KGB Amalrik Yields, Accepts Exile." The writer, Andrei Amalrik, who wrote *Involuntary Journey to Siberia*, was best known for his long essay entitled, "Will the Soviet Union Survive Until 1984?" which the paper described as "a grim portrait of a grim society whose stagnation exposes it to the prospect of violent revolution and war with China."

In it Amalrik predicts the Soviet regime will collapse sometime between 1980 and 1985.

Out in the Orient, on a steel pillar, the Japanese had erected a twenty-ton rock in front of the City Hall in Shiki, a suburb of Tokyo. The monument was an image to emptiness (*International Herald Tribune*, February 26, 1976). Typical of many Japanese were Taro and Hanako Suzuki, who said, "Despite apparent prosperity, people are irritable and restless" (*U.S. News and World Report*, January 7, 1974).

Fear and perplexity seemed to affect most of the world. Back in the U.S., Secretary of the Treasury Simon told the Commonwealth Club in San Francisco, "Malignant forces . . . are subtly, quietly, but very busily eating away at the foundations of our society. . . . One of the saddest experiences in public life is to see businessmen trooping to Washington day after day, hat in hand, seeking shelter from the storm, under a government umbrella" (*Los Angeles Times*,).

While craving freedom, many were driven by fears to seek security in someone whose wisdom or power would be greater than their own. Men as prominent as Paul Henri Spaak was quoted as saying, "Send us a man who can hold the allegiance of all the people, and whether he be God or devil we will receive him" (*Moody Monthly*, March 1974).

Spaak served as first president of the Council of Europe. He was one of the planners of the European Common Market, a former president of the U.N. General Assembly, Secretary-General of NATO, Minister of Foreign Affairs in Belgium, Prime Minister of his nation. If men like Paul Henri Spaak could say, "Give us a man . . . be he God or devil," would others echo the same sentiment?

From the bookshelf, I took a copy of Dostoevsky's *The Brothers Karamazov*. In it I found an intriguing conversation between the devil and Ivan Karamazov. The devil tells him, "All that must be destroyed is the idea of God in mankind. . . . Once humanity has renounced God . . . the man-god will make his appearance" (p. 763, Penguin edition).

And once this demonic god-man appears and gains control, men will have no secrets or privacy, and no liberty to make rules for their homes and families. Men will be forced to work. They will be allowed to believe in witchcraft and sorcery, but churches will be burned. Man will be given the liberty to sin and promised earthly bread.

After listening to the devil tell him all of this, Ivan merely says, "That's, I'm afraid, what our modern Russia is like" (p. 764).

The Beast

Dostoesvky showed man under a satanic ruler whom he called "a beast." I thought of St. John who also describes the last world dictator as a "beast." In Revelation 13:1, he writes, "And I stood upon the sand of the sea and saw a beast rise up out of the sea."

"Interesting," I thought, "how much of prophecy is written in symbolism. It is indeed like 'treasure hidden in a field,' but not so deeply buried but that it can be found by those who dig for it."

To properly interpret the Book of Revelation we must

remember that it was written in a kind of code to a church under persecution. This means that we should be alert to the possibility that some of the words St. John uses are symbolical. So, with the case of a beast rising out of the sea, we may see the beast as symbolic of a world ruler who would blaspheme God, and the sea out of which he rises as symbolic of the masses of people.

Daniel, like John, wrote in an apocalyptic way about the course of history and the end of the world. He too foresaw a final world dictator about whom he was in mourning three full weeks (Dan. 10:2). The dictator would work deceitfully by coming peacefully to obtain his power by flattery (11:21, 23). He will exercise his power through military might and "speak marvelous things against the God of Gods" (11:31-38). But this final world dictator, this beast, will also have complete control of the world's fiscal affairs (11:43).

St. John says, furthermore, that he will cancel the old currencies of the nations and even cause gold to be no longer of value in trade (Rev. 18:11-17). In that day it will certainly be as James says in his epistle, "Go to now, ye rich men, weep and howl for your miseries that shall come upon you. Your riches are corrupted, and your garments are motheaten. Your gold and silver is cankered; and the rust of them shall be a witness against you, and shall eat your flesh as it were fire" (James 5:1-3).

Who Cries Alas?

At that point those financiers who were willing to sacrifice the small businessman's interests and the private rights of individuals are the ones who will cry most bitterly. They will have used their power and wealth to form a world government and to elect a dictator. But he will cleverly cancel their wealth in his new system.

Then the new world money system will be fully established. John tells how this world leader will cause everyone, "both small and great, rich and poor, free and bond, to receive a mark in their right hand, or in their foreheads: And that no man might buy or sell, save he that had the mark" (Rev. 13:16, 17).

The prophet John explains the fearful significance of this mark. "If any man . . . receive his mark in his forehead or in his hand, the same shall drink of the wine of the wrath of God" (Rev. 14:9, 10).

But to the true believers Paul the Apostle writes, "God hath not appointed us to wrath" (1 Thess. 5:9).

John in declaring God's promise to the church says, "I also will keep thee from the hour of temptation which shall come upon all the world" (Rev. 3:10). And Peter says, "The Lord knoweth how to deliver the godly out of temptations and to reserve the unjust unto the day of judgment to be punished" (2 Pet. 2:9).

Christ tells how the true Christians will be removed from the scene of judgment and tells how "one shall be taken and the other left" (Matt. 24:40-42). Christ likened this period to the time of Lot.

I turned in my Bible to Genesis, Chapter 19 and read how the angel said to Lot, "Haste thee, escape thither; for I cannot do anything till thou be come thither (Gen. 19:22). And I read further, "the same day that Lot went out of Sodom it rained brimstone from heaven and destroyed them all. Even thus shall it be when the Son of Man shall be revealed. (Luke 17:29, 30).

"How great is God's mercy," I said as I turned back to Genesis and read, "While he [Lot] lingered the men [angels] laid hold upon his hand, and upon the hand of his wife, and upon the hand of his two daughters; the Lord being merciful unto him: and they brought them forth and set them without the city" (Gen. 19:16).

Just as God delivered Lot and his family from the scene of

115

judgment, so Jesus, in predicting the coming time of tribulation, said, "Pray always that ye may be accounted worthy to escape all these things that shall come to pass" (Luke 21:36).

But, what about those who are not worthy? Christ in describing the end of the age and coming judgment said, "Because iniquity shall abound the love of many shall wax cold" (Matt. 24:12). Paul says, "Now the spirit speaketh expressly in the latter time some shall depart from the faith" (1 Tim. 4:1).

Those who are unworthy of God's deliverance must enter the tribulation period and then choose their final destiny by choosing Christ or Antichrist. And while this reign of evil runs its brief but awful course, many will choose to accept truth and die for their faith, rather than take the mark of the satanic leader, who Paul says will finally be destroyed "with the brightness of Christ's coming" (2 Thess. 2:8).

Man's Hope

The prophet John speaks of this as man's *hope*. When Satan seems to have gained open control of the earth, when he would seek to impose his mark of doom on all, then God gives the command for His Son, Christ, to overthrow the government of Satan, and as John writes, "We give thanks, O Lord God Almighty, which art, and wast, and art to come; because thou hast taken to thee thy great power and hast reigned" (Rev. 11:17).

Jesus will reward the faithful who have stood against the beast and refused his mark. In that glorious hour Satan's kingdom will be utterly and completely destroyed and his role as prince of the earth will end. For Christ will come "to destroy them which destroy the earth" (Rev. 11:18).

Satan, who in the beginning led rebellion in the heavens in his desire to be "like the Most High," sought to lead rebellious men as well, in establishing himself as master of the world. But his rebellion, and ours, were doomed from the

116

start. Jesus is the true master of the world and, one day, every knee will bow to acknowledge that fact.

I closed the Bible and laid it reverently on the desk. For me another day had ended, but the journey of life was not the dismal march to death described by infidels of the ages, rather "the path of the just is as a shining light, that shineth more and more unto the perfect day" (Prov. 4:18).

"Thank God," I said, as I left my study, "that day is drawing closer. The true master of the world will return."

Chapter 8
One Master

I awakened early to the sound of church bells ringing in the distance. Birds in the nearby trees were singing, and the sun was telling me it was time to arise and join the countless numbers who would praise God on this Sunday morning because they knew He reigned supreme. In spite of the forces of darkness that had swept over the earth, the light of faith has not gone out.

America, I thought, has been especially blessed because most of her leaders, in spite of their many human failures, acknowledged God. Let's take a quick roll call of them. All of their quotes were collected from various sources by Benjamin Weiss in his book, *God in American History*.

Benjamin Franklin said, "The longer I live, the more convincing proofs I see that God governs the affairs of men. I therefore beg leave to move that, henceforth, prayers imploring the assistance of heaven be held in this assembly every morning" (Weiss, p. 39).

George Washington, on April 30, 1789, referred to "That

Almighty Being who rules the universe . . . and the Invisible Hand that conducts the affairs of men" (p. 51).

Thomas Jefferson, on March 4, 1805, said, "I shall need the favor of that Being in whose hands we are, who led our fathers, as Israel of old" (p. 58).

James Monroe, in his inaugural address on March 4, 1825, spoke of God's overruling providence, and added, "Except the Lord keep the city, the watchman waketh in vain" (p. 68).

Andrew Jackson, on March 4, 1833, said, "It is my most fervent prayer to that Almighty Being . . . that He will overrule all my intentions and actions" (p. 73).

James Knox Polk, in his inaugural address on March 4, 1845, said, ". . . I fervently invoke the aid of that Almighty Ruler of the Universe in whose hands are the destinies of nations" (p. 80).

Franklin Pierce, on March 4, 1853, acknowledged, "dependence upon God and His overruling providence" (p. 86).

Abraham Lincoln, on April 30, 1863, spoke of "devoutly recognizing the Supreme Authority and just government of Almighty God in all the affairs of men and nations" (p. 92).

Rutherford B. Hayes, on March 5, 1877, said he was "Looking for the guidance of that Divine Hand by which the destinies of nations and individuals are shaped" (p. 103).

Grover Cleveland, on March 4, 1885, said, "Let us not trust to human effort alone, but humbly acknowledge the power and goodness of Almighty God who presides over the destiny of nations. . . . I know there is a Supreme Being who rules the affairs of men" (p. 109).

Benjamin Harrison prayed for "favor and help from Almighty God" (p. 110).

William McKinley said on March 4, 1897, "Our faith teaches that there is no safer reliance than upon the God of our fathers" (p. 115).

Theodore Roosevelt, in assuming office of president, on March 4, 1901, said, "I reverently invoke for my guidance the direction and favor of Almighty God" (p. 116).

William Howard Taft, on March 4, 1909, said, "I invoke the aid of Almighty God" (p. 120).

Woodrow Wilson, on March 4, 1913 and 1917, recognized God in such expressions as "God's own presence . . . God helping me . . . in God's Providence . . . I pray God that I may be given wisdom" (p. 125).

Warren Harding, on March 4, 1921, asked, "What doth the Lord require of thee but to do justly and to love mercy, and to walk humbly with thy God?" (p. 126).

Calvin Coolidge, on March 4, 1925, spoke of cherishing "no purpose save to merit the favor of Almighty God" (p. 131).

Herbert Hoover, on assuming office as president on March 4, 1929, said, "I ask the help of Almighty God in this service" (p. 132).

Franklin Delano Roosevelt recognized God in all of his inaugural addresses. On March 4, 1933, he said, "We humbly ask the blessing of God." On January 20, 1937, he said, "I shall do my utmost . . . seeking Divine guidance." On January 20, 1941, he said, "We go forward in the service of our country by the will of God." January 20, 1945, he said, "We pray to Him now for the vision to see our way clearly" (pp. 137-138).

Harry S. Truman, who made many references to God and quotations from the Scriptures, said on January 20, 1949, "With God's help the future of mankind will be assured in a world of justice, harmony and peace" (p. 141).

Dwight D. Eisenhower, in his inaugural address on January 21, 1957, said, "Before all else, we seek upon our common labor as a nation, the blessings of Almighty God" (p. 145).

John Fitzgerald Kennedy said, on January 20, 1961, "The

rights of man come not from the generosity of the state but from the hand of God" (p. 146).

Lyndon B. Johnson, who made frequent references to God in his speeches, said on January 20, 1965, "If we fail now . . . we will have forgotten that democracy rests on faith" (p. 151).

Richard Milhous Nixon, on January 20, 1969, said, "Let us go forward firm in our faith . . . sustained by our confidence in the will of God" (p. 154).

Gerald R. Ford, when assuming office on August 9, 1974, said, "I ask you to confirm me as your president with your prayers . . . God helping me, I will not let you down" (p. 158).

Senator Mark Hatfield moved that the Senate pass a resolution calling for a national day of humiliation and fasting and prayer. The motion carried with no opposition. The resolution read, in part, "It behooves us to humble ourselves before Almighty God, to confess our national sins and to pray for clemency and forgiveness."

Back to God

In the mid-seventies, there was without question evidence that many people were returning with greater fervor to the faith of their fathers. A headline out of Washington told of an amendment for school prayer that had been supported at a Senate hearing. Spread across six columns of the *San Jose Mercury* (January 16, 1976) was a headline reading, "Creation Gets Equal Billing in School Texts." In the *Los Angeles Times* (February 11, 1975), John Dart wrote an article boldly proclaiming that the "decline of religion may have ended."

A six column headline in the *International Herald Tribune* (April 22, 1976) stated that "Scientific Research Revives Question of Life after Death." It quoted the noted psychiatrist Dr. Elizabeth Kubler-Ross, whose "talks with hundreds of persons who had been resuscitated had convinced her 'beyond a shadow of a doubt' that there is life after death."

From Stuttgart, Germany, came news that world-wide Bible distribution was soaring. In 1975 Bible distribution was up forty percent over any previous year. The United Bible Societies had sold or given away 44,766,000 Bibles and 248,000,000 portions of the Bible. Dr. Ulrich Fick explained that this phenomenal increase was partially due to the increasing cooperation between the Bible societies and the Roman Catholic Church.

Even in the Soviet Union, the anti-God Communist leaders were failing to stamp out all reference to God. A headline from the *Los Angeles Times* reads, "Faith Persists Among Russians Despite State." The article went on to say that "party vigilantes often stand outside functioning churches to question unknown visitors and to discourage young people from attending."

But their efforts to discourage the young have not been successful. From personal contact, I knew this to be true. In Detroit, Michigan, I spent three days with Fred Smolchuk, who had dared to spend twenty-one days behind the Iron Curtain, not as a tourist receiving the official conducted tour with the crowd, but as an individual alone. Fred was met by the KGB on his arrival, interrogated and warned not to visit the villages. He was told if he wished to see his relatives who lived in rural areas, they must come to the city for he could not go to them. When friends came to his hotel in the city, they said, "Let's go outside for here the walls are listening."

Fred returned home from his travels in Russia with news that both saddened and encouraged him. Some were so eager to have a Bible they would offer as much as two months' wages for one copy of the Bible. And in the meetings of the Christian believers, which were often held in secret, those in attendance were not only the very old and very young, but in many cases the majority were young married couples. But in the classrooms, the Communist teachers faced their greatest problems. Here the Russian educators were becoming increasingly frustrated by students, who were supposed to be brain-washed atheists, asking openly to discuss God and the immortality of the soul. When the teachers objected to such questions the students would point to Western astronauts, like Borman, Lovell, and Anders, of Apollo 8, who read the Bible from their space craft for the whole world to hear. Or they would refer to Buzz Aldren who partook of the Sacrament on the moon.

Not every Soviet youth was deaf to Christian testimonies of men like Cernan of Apollo 17, who talked of God the creator, and a universe that did not happen by chance (*Los Angeles Times*, December 21, 1972). Some undoubtedly knew the testimony of Jim Irwin. When astronaut Colonel Jim Irwin had been to the moon, he returned to tell the world "that experience has to change a person inside. It has to make a man appreciate the creation of God, the love of God, and the infinite precision with which He controls everything in outer space, and, of course, everything here on earth, too" (Ole Anthony, *Crossfire*, p. 129).

"If the Russian students are too persistent," said Fred Smolchuk, "they may pay a bitter penalty for their questions."

But apparently some were willing to pay a price in their honest search for truth. The youth of Russia were not fully persuaded that the message of materialism was enough. They were beginning to ask again, "Is man mud, mind, or matter; devil or angel?" They knew that one of Russia's intellectuals, Aleksandr Solzhenitsyn, had been banished from the Soviet for daring to express his views. And as millions over the world listened to this man called "The

Conscience of Russia," they heard him speak of his faith in God, and refer to God the creator.

Scientists Acknowledge God

Merlin Grant, who taught math, physics, and astronomy in well-known universities, said, "God is not only creator He is sovereign" (Monsma, p. 147). Claud Hathaway, the designer of the electronic brain for the National Advisory Committee on Aeronautics, says, "Although my knowledge of God in earlier days was based more on reason, I now rest largely on the experience of knowing Him inwardly and personally" (Monsma, p. 143). Donald Robert Carr, research scientist of Columbia University, who was associated with J.C. Kulp in authoring *Dating with Natural Radio Active Carbon*, writes, "By divine Grace I have this spiritual faith. It then becomes a case of the Spirit Himself bearing witness with my spirit that I am a child of God" (Monsma, p. 132).

Robert Morris Page, the famous physicist and inventor of pulsation radar, who had won numerous scientific awards, said, "The authenticity of the writings of these men is established by such things as the prediction of highly significant events far in the future that could be accomplished only through knowledge obtained from a realm which is not subject to the laws of time as we know them. One of the great evidences is the long series of prophecies concerning Jesus the Messiah. The prophecies extended for hundreds of years prior to the birth of Christ" (Monsma, p. 29).

Prophecies Concerning Jesus the Messiah

It interested me greatly that a scientist and physicist so world renowned as Robert Morris Page would view the prophecies made concerning Jesus the Messiah, and conclude that they were supernatural. He was not alone in this conviction. Other men of scientific minds had studied the writings of the prophets and discovered the same.

125

Over seven centuries before He was born, the prophet Micah wrote concerning the place of His birth. "But, thou, Bethlehem Ephratah, though thou be little among the thousands of Judah, yet out of thee shall he come forth unto me that is to be ruler in Israel; whose goings forth have been from of old, from everlasting" (Micah 5:2).

And about fifty years before Micah named Bethlehem as the place of His birth, Isaiah wrote concerning His virgin birth. "Therefore the Lord himself shall give you a sign; Behold, a virgin shall conceive, and bear a son, and shall call his name Immanuel" (Isa. 7:14).

Isaiah also prophesied His suffering and its meaning. "With his stripes we are healed" (Isaiah 53:5). And seven centuries later, Matthew wrote: "He healed all that were sick: that it might be fulfilled which was spoken by Esaias [Isaiah] the prophet" (Matt. 8:17).

When Jesus commenced His public ministry, Luke tells how He entered the synagogue at Nazareth and quoted from the prophecies of Isaiah, "The Spirit of the Lord is upon me because he has anointed me to preach the gospel to the poor" (Luke 4:18). When He closed the book at the conclusion of the reading He said, "This day is this scripture fulfilled in your ears" (Luke 4:21).

Matthew tells how Judas bargained for his betrayal, saying, "What will ye give me, and I will deliver him unto you? And they convenanted with him for thirty pieces of silver" (Matt. 26:15). Almost five centuries earlier, the prophet Zechariah described this event, "If ye think good, give me my price; so they weighed for my price thirty pieces of silver" (Zech. 11:12).

His Suffering

Isaiah wrote of Christ, "I gave my back to the smiters, and my cheeks to them that plucked off the hair: I hid not my face from shame and spitting" (Isa. 50:6). And centuries later

126

Mark wrote, "And some began to spit upon him, and to cover his face, and to buffet him . . . and strike him with the palms of their hands" (Mark 14:65).

The Psalmist wrote: "They pierced my hands and my feet" (Ps. 22:16). And the writers of the Gospels described the crucifixion when they pierced His hands and feet.

They Parted His Garments Among Them

In the same Psalm, we read, "They part my garments among them, and cast lots upon my vesture" (Ps. 22:18).

And Mark describes the scene at the cross: "When they had crucified him, they parted his garments, casting lots upon them" (Mark 15:24).

Isaiah spoke of his burial by saying, "He made his grave with the . . . rich" (Isa. 53:9). And Matthew tells how "a rich man of Arimathaea named Joseph . . . when he had taken the body . . . he laid it in his own new tomb" (Matt. 27:57-60).

David wrote concerning the Messiah, "Thou wilt not suffer thine Holy One to see corruption" (Ps. 16:10). Hundreds of years later, Peter, who had personally seen Christ physically raised from the dead recognized that David had prophesied the event in those brief, enigmatic words. He said, "Men and brethren, let me freely speak unto you of the patriarch David, that he is both dead and buried, and his sepulchre is with us unto this day. Therefore being a prophet, and knowing that God had sworn with an oath to him, that of the fruit of his loins, according to the flesh, he would raise up Christ to sit on his throne; He seeing this before spake of the resurrection of Christ, that his soul was not left in hell, neither his flesh did see corruption" (Acts 2:29-31).

Regarding his ascension, the Psalmist wrote, "Thou hast ascended on high, thou hast led captivity captive: thou has received gifts for men" (Psalm 68:18). And after his resurrection and ascension, Paul wrote, "When he ascended up on high he led captivity captive and gave gifts unto men" (Eph. 4:8).

Over Three Hundred Prophecies

Some who studied the writings of the prophets of old estimated conservatively that over three hundred utterances had been given which described each detail of Christ's birth, life, death, resurrection, and ascension. After his resurrection, Christ walked on the road to Emmaus (Luke 24:13-35) with Cleophas and a friend. Jesus asked, "What manner of communications are these that ye have one to another as ye walk and are sad?" The men did not recognize Jesus, for Luke says, "Their eyes were holden that they should not know him." The men told Christ about the death of Jesus on the cross and said, "We trusted that it had been he which should have redeemed Israel." Then Jesus said unto them, "O fools, and slow of heart to believe all that the prophets had spoken: Ought not Christ to have suffered these things, and to enter into his glory? And beginning at Moses and all the prophets, he expounded unto them in all scriptures the things concerning himself."

One of the most common phrases associated with the ministry of Jesus as recorded in the Gospels was "that it might be fulfilled which was spoken by the prophet" (e.g. Matt. 12:17). As I turned the pages of the Gospels, I counted more than a score of such phrases.

When certain men were sent to arrest Jesus, they returned saying "never man spake like this man" (John 7:46). I remembered quoting these words on the club grounds of Lucknow, India, when conversing with some young Hindu students.

"Do you believe that Christ was a teacher in this world," I asked.

"Yes," they replied, "we believe He was."

"Was He a good man?"

And to this question, they agreed.

"Must a good man tell the truth?" I continued.

"Yes," they answered, "a man must tell the truth if he is a good man."

"If he were a liar," I continued, "you could not say he was good?"

And they nodded their heads in agreement.

"Then," I continued, "will you consider the words of Jesus and the statements He made concerning Himself?"

How startled His listeners must have been when He said "Verily, verily, I say unto you, Before Abraham was, I am" (John 8:58). On another occasion some turned away from Christ when He said, "I came down from heaven, not to do my own will but the will of him that sent me" (John 6:38). Christ asked, "Doth this offend you. What if he shall see the Son of man ascend up where he was before?" (John 6:61, 62).

On another occasion, Jesus said, "I go to prepare a place for you, And if I go and prepare a place for you, I will come again" (John 14:2, 3). Over and over again, Christ spoke of His return. He said, "For the Son of man shall come in the glory of his Father with his angel; then shall he reward every man according to his works" (Matt. 16:27). Jude tells how, "Enoch also, seventh from Adam, prophesied saying, Behold the Lord cometh with ten thousand of his saints to execute judgment upon all" (Jude 14, 15).

What Shall Be the Sign of His Coming?

One day on the Mount of Olives the disciples asked Jesus, "What shall be the sign of thy coming?" (Matt. 24:3). And among the signs that Christ gave, which included wars and violence and iniquity, He said there would be a time of trouble "such as was not since the beginning of the world" (Matt. 24:21).

Many times I had read in Revelation 6, "For the great day

of his wrath is come" (v. 17). The subsequent chapters unfold scenes of sorrow that cause man to truly understand why Christ said it would be a time of trouble unlike anything since the beginning of the world. In the sixteenth chapter of Revelation, where the final stages of Armageddon are described, the prophet tells of the heat of the sun being so intense that men were scorched (v. 9). And in this hour of judgment the prophet says, "There fell noisome and grievous sores upon men" (v. 2). The prophet also tells how the devil arouses the armies of earth to gather in a final battle and how the earth shakes and "the cities of the nations fell" (v. 19).

Could It Be an Atomic War?

I had listened to various scientific groups through the years of the atomic age discuss the possible dangers of an all-out atomic war.

A salvo of atomic bombs detonated in the atmosphere could rupture the thin protective layer of ozone, and allow the deadly rays of the sun to scorch men with a heat and cause sores to break out on their bodies. I had also heard some scientists state that the concussion from bombs exploded in heavens could possibly rock the entire earth on its axis so that cities would be destroyed from the earthquake as well as from bombs.

Isaiah wrote: "And the loftiness of man shall be bowed down, and the haughtiness of men shall be made low: and the Lord alone shall be exalted in that day. . . . And they shall go into the holes of the rocks and into the caves of the earth, for the fear of the Lord and for the glory of his majesty when he ariseth to shake terribly the earth" (2:17, 19).

For thirty years I had not only studied the prophecies of the Bible and committed many chapters to memory, but had also attended prophetic conferences conducted by men of faith in many lands. I had sat with the finest scholars of the

Word, and listened to them in Christian spirit discuss objectively the prophetic truths pertaining to coming judgment on the ungodly and God's marvelous provision for the deliverance of His faithful. They all agreed that the true believers of many centuries had tasted persecution from satanic leaders, but in the coming judgment that would represent God's anger and wrath, God's faithful would be delivered.

He Will Come Suddenly

The prophet Malachi wrote about 397 B.C.: "Behold the day cometh that shall burn as an oven; and all the proud, yea, and all that do wickedly shall burn as stubble" (4:1). The apostle Paul said: "The day of the Lord so cometh as a thief in the night. For when they shall say, Peace and safety; then sudden destruction cometh upon them . . . and they shall not escape" (I Thess. 5:2, 3). The prophet Isaiah agrees with the others and writes: "The multitude of the terrible ones shall be as chaff that passeth away: yea, it shall be at an instant suddenly" (29:5).

When God sends His Son to destroy the rebellious powers of earth suddenly, they shall be swept away like chaff. Daniel tells how these powers on earth are "broken in pieces together, and become like the chaff of the summer threshing floor; and the wind carried them away, that no place was found for them" (2:35).

If the writers of the Bible ceased at this point, then man would be without hope. The bells would ring for this last act, and the curtain of time would drop on earth's stage. With the last light extinguished, the silence would only be broken by the sighing of the radioactive winds sweeping over bomb ruined cities, where the silent cemeteries of earth would point to the graves where faith and hope had been buried.

If Christ does not come and establish a kingdom of peace on earth, then were the prophets deceived and they have

131

filled centuries with their deception. The world they described under a ruling Christ would be nothing more than a concocted dream from kaleidoscopic imaginations.

"Christ would come," I said aloud. "He must come!"

I turned my eyes to the open window as though looking back through the centuries. I thought of the glories of the Caesars. In Rome I had photographed the mute testimony to their faded grandeur on the banks of the Tiber. In the musty monuments of the Pharaohs I had crawled in the pyramids, thinking of Egypt's golden era that had passed. While tourists stood in the Tower of London gazing at crown jewels protected in their encasements of glass and steel, I thought of Weeping Gundulf who built the tower as instructed by King William. While this unusual monk directed the building of Europe's oldest fortress, he wept while he worked. Possibly he foresaw the suffering of the kings who would languish in the tragic Tower, and of the queens and princes whose heads would fall beneath the executioner's axe.

Few royal heads were adorned with costlier jewels than those of the Russian Tsars. The imperial crown carried more than 4,000 karats of diamonds of the first water, and a summit cross of diamonds and rubies worth fifty-two million dollars. The imperial scepter was surmounted with the world-famous Orloff diamond containing 189 karats and valued at thirty million dollars. But even they could not ransom Nicholas, Alexandra and their children from bloody slaughter.

History points painfully to such tragedies as those of honest Abe Lincoln and young President Kennedy, who fell from assassins' bullets, and Willie Brandt who was betrayed by a so-called friend, and forced to leave his office as Chancellor of Germany. Richard Nixon's theme was "let's put it all together," but the scandal of Watergate tore his good intentions apart.

Henry Kissinger, once called in high circles "Secretary of the World," made statements that were underlined with heavy emphasis on the front pages of the European press. He said, "I think of myself as a historian more than a statesman. As a historian, you have to be conscious of the fact that every civilization that has ever existed has ultimately collapsed" (*International Herald Tribune*, April 4, 1976).

If Christ does not return, then man faces a future devoid of hope.

The Blessed Hope

But if the prophets speak the truth, man has a hope. Paul wrote to Titus: "Looking for that blessed hope, and glorious appearing of the great God and our Saviour Jesus Christ" (2:13). Peter says, "Be ready to give an answer to every man who asketh you a reason of the hope that is in you" (1 Pet. 3:15).

And how did Peter reason? He looked at the more than 300 prophecies which had been literally fulfilled in Christ's first coming, and knew the 1500 prophecies concerning His second coming to rule and reign would also be fulfilled in the same manner.

The prophecies were not merely inferential statements, they were bold, they were clear. Daniel said: "I saw. . . one like the Son of man come with clouds of heaven, . . . and there was given him dominion and glory and a kingdom, that all people, nations and languages should serve him: his dominion is an everlasting dominion which shall never pass away and his kingdom . . . shalt not be destroyed" (7:13, 14).

Peace At Last

I closed my eyes and asked myself what our world would be like if it could have peace? In the Soviet alone, over four million men could take off the uniforms of war and don the clothing of peace. The nations of the world could take the $350 billion spent annually on arms and armies and feed the hungry. The factories making weapons of destruction could make implements of peace. And the fearful tax burdens borne by those paying interest on war debts would be no longer. Was it only a dream? Or was it a hope with foundation? Would He come? And would He bring peace?

Zechariah said, "He shall speak peace . . . and his dominion shall be even . . . to the ends of the earth" (9:10). Isaiah said, "Of the increase of his government and peace there shall be no end" (9:6).

While some said that the world had grown too small to accommodate her children, others pointed to a map of the world and asked, "How can this be?" All of the cities of the world cover about one percent of earth's land surface, which is 58 million square miles. If one multiplied that area of land by the number of acres per square mile, it would offer every human being almost ten acres each. Everybody in today's world could find standing room in the buildings of New York City.

The earth still has room and Christ's words still stand: "Seek ye first the kingdom of God and his righteousness and all these things shall be added unto you" (Matt. 6:33).

Christ not only told this to others, He demonstrated this truth in His own life. He did not look like a beggar. The seamless robe He wore to the cross was one of the finest garments men could wear. And when the multitude was hungry, He fed all who were present. He declared that God's laws would never change, even though heaven and earth would pass away.

Was it accidental or coincidental that the founding fathers discovered America with her wealth and abundance? Or did God direct the paths of those who were willing to seek first the kingdom of God and His righteousness.

Governor William Bradford told that when the Pilgrims landed at Plymouth Rock, "they fell on their knees and blessed the God of Heaven Who had brought them" (Weiss, p. 26).

"I wonder," I asked myself, "just how many states in the Union have acknowledged God in their Constitutions or mottoes?" I began leafing through the pages of Benjamin Weiss's excellent book (*God in American History*) and found that every one of our fifty states, from Alabama to Wyoming, had indeed acknowledged God in one or the other. Nor were these statements of gratitude to and trust in the Almighty simply the pious platitudes of an older, more credulous generation.

Public concern for expression of thanks and petition to God was evident in 1954, when both the Senate and the House of Representatives approved a joint resolution calling for the establishment of a "room with facilities for prayer and meditation for the use of Members of the Senate and House of Representatives." I have visited that prayer room personally. An open Bible lies on an altar, and a stained glass window depicts George Washington kneeling in prayer. Under this scene were the words of the sixteenth Psalm, which read, "Preserve me, O God; for in thee do I put my trust."

Do today's lawmakers actually come into this room to pray? Mr. Miller, the Keeper of the House, told me of the occasions when he had seen legislators enter the room and with bowed knees and upturned faces petition God for help and guidance.

One of the most visited monuments in the nation's capital is the Washington Monument, standing over 555 feet high. Many times I had glanced up at the marble pyramid that sits atop that obelisk with its aluminum cap. Inscribed on that cap are the words, "Praise be to God." And, inside the hollow monument carved tribute blocks line the stairway. On these one may read:

> SUFFER THE LITTLE CHILDREN TO COME UNTO ME AND FORBID THEM NOT; FOR SUCH IS THE KINGDOM OF GOD
>
> Luke 18:16.

> TRAIN UP A CHILD IN THE WAY HE SHOULD GO: AND WHEN HE IS OLD, HE WILL NOT DEPART FROM IT
>
> Proverbs 22:6

> SEARCH THE SCRIPTURES
>
> John 5:39; Acts 17:11

> HOLINESS UNTO THE LORD
>
> Exodus 28:36; 39:30; Zechariah 14:20

> IN GOD WE TRUST

> GOD AND OUR NATIVE LAND

> MAY HEAVEN TO THIS UNION CONTINUE ITS BENEFICENCE

Whenever we sing the fourth stanza of the Star Spangled Banner, we "praise the Power that hath made and preserved us as a nation! . . . and this be our motto, In God is our trust!"

In spite of their failures one thing should be said of America's leaders: with remarkably few exceptions they have been God-fearing people.

"If God's laws are true," I said aloud, "then it may be understandable why our forefathers were led to this land of abundance."

In my earlier years in the U.S.A., I had driven the 2,000 mile coast line from Maine to Florida, and then the 1,600 mile journey along the waters of America's Gulf Coast. I had driven repeatedly along the Pacific Coast from San Diego to Seattle, and had stood on the northern shores of Alaska. In all, the nation boasts 11,000 miles of coastline. Alaska alone can net in a single year over $90 million from its fish.

The state of Iowa could reap 800 million bushels of corn in a year, and Kansas 300 million bushels of wheat. The hardwood forests of Arkansas could provide paychecks annually of a half a billion dollars. And neighboring southern states would yield 10 million bales of cotton. California in a normal season would yield $3 billion worth of fruit and vegetables, not to mention the livestock of the ranchlands, the gold and silver, and timber and oil.

The Earth Is Full of Thy Riches

Some who studied the riches of earth estimated the combined value of the gold and silver, the grain and oil and timber, the fish and fruit and minerals, etc., at one decillion dollars. This figure, of course, was beyond my comprehension, but slowly I repeated, "Million, billion, trillion, quadrillion, quintillion, sextillion, septillion, octillion, novillion, decillion!" Taking pen and paper, I divided the four billion of earth's population into this figure, and saw that everyone would be a billionaire, if he shared such wealth. Such a suggestion sounds foolish under our present system, but under some other system there might be at least plenty for all.

The psalmist said, "The earth is full of thy riches" (104:24). With renewed interest, I turned again to the Bible to see what God's prophets wrote concerning earth's riches.

In reading the Scriptures it was very apparent that God wanted man to know that He, God, was the rightful owner of earth. The writers of the Psalms recognized this truth and repeated it frequently in such words as: "The earth is the Lord's and the fulness thereof; the world and they that dwell therein" (24:1). Or "every beast of the forest is mine, the cattle upon a thousand hills . . . for the world is mine and the fulness thereof" (50:10, 12).

God indeed had a rightful claim on the earth as creator, and a claim that was enhanced as He sustained life upon the planet. He was the only true money master of the world who could say "the silver is mine, and the gold is mine saith the Lord of hosts" (Hag. 2:8).

If God owned earth's riches, what claim did man have on the world's wealth? David said that God had made man a little lower than the angels and had given him dominion over the earth. Lucifer had that position before he fell, but in rebelling against God, he lost his claim.

I pondered once more Ezekiel's description of Satan: "Thou hast been in Eden the garden of God. . . . Thou wast perfect from the day that thou wast created, till iniquity was found in thee. . . . Thou hast defiled thy sanctuaries . . . I will bring thee to ashes upon the earth" (28:13, 15, 17, 18).

Satan forfeited his position when he fell, and God in turn offered man the dominion over earth. Why God has delayed the final judgment for Lucifer, we may not fully know, but one thing is made clear in the Scriptures. When the time comes for God to judge him, He will also judge man.

That's really why Christ came, to rescue man from judgment. It had always been in the character of God to have mercy in the midst of judgment. That's why He clothed Adam and Eve after He expelled them from the garden, and that's why He put a mark on Cain when He sentenced him to a nomadic life. It was a mark of protection, of mercy.

Judgment and Mercy and Faith

"How fearful and yet how wonderful!" I thought. In Christ stern righteousness and merciful peace have kissed each other in complete fulfillment of the will of God (Ps. 85:10). Christ often reminded His followers, directly and in parables, that He would one day come in glory and demand of men an account of their stewardship on His behalf. Certainly the true money master of the world would have to require an accounting from His servants. Thus were judgment and mercy brought together in this one man who suffered and died on the cross, was buried, and raised from the dead. And when His disciples saw Him risen from the dead and were themselves clothed with the power of the Holy Spirit, they began zealously to obey His final command, to preach the gospel to every creature. It was, and is, an enormous task and one wonders at the faith men need in order to begin to do it.

The aroma of freshly brewed coffee drifting through the open door of my study attracted me to the dining room, where I found Verna ready to ring the breakfast bell. An hour later, we sat in the congregation listening to Rev. James Boulware deliver his Sunday morning message on the great commission, using as his text, "Go ye into all the world and preach the gospel to every creature" (Mark 16:15).

As I glanced across the aisle, I saw Dr. George Flattery and his wife, Esther. Dr. Flattery, the president of International Correspondence Institute, did not feel that the great commission was impossible. Tens of thousands in many lands were receiving the message of Christ, and were being trained for leadership through the program of the International Correspondence Institute.

On this particular Sunday, he was surrounded by some of the directors who had flown in from their respective fields. Vern Warner in the opening part of the service had told of the spiritual awakening across South America. Norm Correll gave a similar report from Africa. Bob Hoskins spoke of the hundreds of thousands in the Arab-speaking world who had enrolled in the ICI courses which explained God's plan of salvation through Christ.

Paul Pipkin was also present. Tens of thousands in the

Orient had been reached through his efforts. I had met Paul first in San Francisco in 1945, when he was leaving for China. Even with the nation on the verge of the Communist takeover, he moved into Peking where their first child was born. A dozen years later Paul visited our studios in Los Angeles, where we were producing a weekly telecast, covering half of the nation. He told of his relationship with the Far East Broadcasting Company in the Philippines. We were thrilled to learn the F.E.B.C., with its many stations, was capable of giving the gospel message to three-quarters of the globe.

When Christ gave the great commission, He surely knew that along with exploding population, "knowledge would be increased," and man would have media to fulfill His command. Through the voice of radio alone, the world can hear the message of Christ being proclaimed more than 400,000 hours each year. The Iron and Bamboo Curtains are ineffective barriers to the voice of radio which penetrates into the very heart of Communist territories.

As the minister continued to speak about fulfilling the great commission, I thought of the countless dedicated men at home who were devoted to this task. A few years previously at a National Religious Broadcasters Convention, I had heard some express fears that radio and television stations of America would eventually close their channels to the proclamation of the message of Christ. But, in contrast to such pessimistic predictions, the circumstances of the present seemed gloriously bright. When I visited Jim Bakker of Trinity Broadcasting, he showed me close to a hundred letters from leading American television stations asking for their program, known as "The PTL Club."

When Jim spoke of their telecast carried on scores of the nation's stations, he said with deep emotion, "Our great desire is to give the gospel, not just to America, but to the

One Master

world." His contribution to foreign missions proved his sincerity.

Surely on this very Sunday, God had many faithful witnesses. The pastor concluded his morning message by reminding his audience that Christ would reward His faithful now, and in a new heaven, and a new earth, and a holy city (Rev. 21).

One in Spirit

After the service friends returned to our apartment for lunch. As we relaxed in the living room following the meal, I smiled at the contrasting personalities of our guests. They were Fred, son of a Dutch banker, Bob, an academician for a quarter of a century, and John from Norway.

In the course of the conversation, Bob asked, "How are you progressing with your book, *Money Master of the World?*

"I'm almost finished, Bob," I replied.

"Are you going to tell us who the money master of the world is?" asked Fred.

"Certainly," I replied. "It is Christ."

As John nodded for me to continue, I said, "My book is an honest effort to view the events of the past and the prospects for tomorrow in the light of Bible prophecy. Without that light one might hear a man as brilliant as Robert Ingersol say, 'Life is a dark barren vale between the ice-clad peaks of two cold eternities.' Not everyone today, of course, will accept the message of the prophets of the Bible. There seems to be a polarizing of views. Scoffers increasingly reject the Scriptures and turn more to the lusts of the flesh, but those who accept the teachings of Christ are growing daily in strength and numbers."

"God has promised," said John, "that in the last days He would pour out His Spirit upon all flesh, and the same Spirit that brings us together will lead us into truth."

141

"But," asked Fred, "why do you choose as a title for your book, *Money Master of the World?*"

Glancing at the clock, I said, "I remember when Arthur Godfrey was asked the time, and he replied, 'Do you want me to tell you the time of day or give you the history of the watch?' No, I won't give you the history of the watch or the whole story, but in a few sentences my book format is this: Men today are afraid of their financial future. They find that their destiny seems to be in the hands of powers they cannot control. From the Bible we show that these powers include Satan who seeks to control the world in a form of world government described by the prophets. This government under Satan is described also by writers like Dostoyevsky of Russia, who in his novel *The Brothers Karamazov*, seems to leave mankind hopelessly in the hands of Satan. He speaks of satanic world rulers who hold in their hands man's conscience and his bread. The leader of this world government will have unprecedented powers. According to the prophets, he will control both the military and the monetary establishments. He will have cancelled the old money systems, and will seek to mark men with his mark, before any can buy or sell. Such a ruler will have the appearance of being the money master of the world. But he is not.

"God declared that Lucifer forfeited his right to rule earth when he sinned against God. And man, who was made a little lower than the angels, was placed in dominion over the new creation. When Satan, who tempts disobedient men and angels to follow him, believes that he has finally gained control of earth, Christ will appear on the scene to destroy them that destroy the earth."

"And," asked Fred, "that is the end?'

"Oh, no, that is just the beginning. With the ending of Lucifer's influence and the destruction of those who followed him, the prophets declare in hundreds of passages that

Christ will establish peace and order on earth. His kingdom, Daniel says, 'Will never be destroyed. And the kingdom shall not be left to other people' (2:44).

"Man has tried through the centuries to bring peace to this world, but a glance at the past shows that every form of government, autocracy, aristocracy, oligarchy, monarchy, and even democracy, has not brought peace to our world. Today more men are echoing the words of England's Prime Minister Gladstone, 'More and more I find my thoughts turning to the great statement, when the Son of man cometh.' "

"So," said Bob, "your book concludes with Christ appearing on the scene and overthrowing Satan, and establishing a kingdom of peace and plenty, and in this role He is the true money master of the world?"

"In brief, that is it."

"It is an interesting study of human nature to see how man will turn to God for help more readily when he has expended his own efforts in a futile search for success."

"I believe you are right, Bob," I replied. "I remember that Tolstoy said, 'For thirty-five years of my life I was in the proper sense a nihilist—not a revolutionary socialist, but a man who believed nothing. Five years ago, I believed in the doctrines of Jesus and my whole life underwent a sudden transformation" (*Are All Great Men Infidels?* p. 12).

"And much the same could be said for Dostoyevsky, can it not?"

"According to Konstantin Mochulsky," I replied, "that is correct. Mochulsky wrote an intriguing introduction to the Bantam edition of *The Brothers Karamozov*. In it he tells of Dostoyevsky's conversion. In 1849 the writer was condemned to death for his revolutionary political activities. He actually went to the scaffold before his sentence was commuted to a term of imprisonment in Siberia. That day on the scaffold, however, something in him died and, later in Siberia, he met Christ."

Maybe what happened to Dostoyevsky will happen to all the world," said John. "It seems that it stands today upon a scaffold. Wars are increasing, pollution is destroying the environment, famine lurks in the corridors, inflation destroys wealth. The world's hopes are being dashed one by one. Let's hope that we may soon reach the day when we sing hosannas to the returning Christ."

"You know, John, I saw something recently that could easily point to the return of Christ—though you might not suspect it at first."

"What's that, Willard?"

"You'll recall, no doubt, that when St. John described the new Jerusalem coming down out of heaven that it measured as a perfect cube. That has always been a bit bewildering to Bible students, since we think of cities as having shapes related to the topography in which they occur. Thus the peculiar shape of Manhattan, London, Tokyo, or Los Angeles."

"You know, Willard, I've always been a little puzzled by that. I have even thought at times that it might have some symbolical meaning, that, for example the cubic shape of the city spoke of its full perfection."

"That's probably true, John, but it's very interesting to note in addition that, with calculations only feasible by computers, men are designing a building two and one-quarter miles high. R. Buckminster Fuller describes on page 350 of his book *Utopia or Oblivion* the tetrahedron-shaped cities which could accommodate as many as a million people, and the height would be approximately the same as the length and width.

"A few years ago man might laugh at such a thought, but one can hardly laugh at a man who has received the Royal

Gold Medal for Architecture awarded by the Queen on the recommendation of the Royal Institute of Architects, and the 1968 Gold Medal award of the National Institute of Arts and Letters.

"And," I might add, "R. Buckminster Fuller was nominated for the 1969 Nobel Peace Prize."

"Didn't Fuller design the geodesic domes that are over the world?"

"Yes, he built them originally to house men on the DEW line spread across the Arctic, but now they can be found in fifty different countries. His credentials are impressive."

After our guests went their various ways, Verna and I went for a stroll in the early evening dusk. While we were out the street lights came on. Men once wondered at the statement of St. John concerning a coming city without night. But, in San Diego, one of America's most respected astronauts described plans for a space platform, with mirrors attached, which could orbit earth and bathe the world night and day with a reflected light from the sun, which would end the need for energy to light the city, and relieve the residents from fear of darkness.

One day there will be no energy shortages. All buildings might be like the new Encon Building, a forty-three-story structure on Third Avenue in New York, where the builders hope to save a million dollars annually in energy costs by drawing directly upon the sun.

For a few moments we walked along in silence. Verna observed that my lips were moving. She asked, "What are you saying?"

"Nothing new," I replied with a smile. "Something you and I have uttered together many times."

Thy kingdom come
Thy will be done
On earth as it is in heaven . . .

For thine is the kingdom
And the power and the glory
Forever
Amen.

As twilight surrendered to darkness, we turned back to our apartment. I meditated on the awesome and wonderful course that mankind had followed through the centuries. The bells of the distant church tower that had greeted me early in the morning were now telling me it was midnight. As I was just about to fall asleep, I silently committed my family, nation, and world to

GOD. THE MASTER OF THE UNIVERSE,
MASTER OF MEN and
MONEY MASTER OF THE WORLD.

EPILOGUE

My grandfather, Peter Cantelon, died at midday on his seventieth birthday. He had worked in the forenoon with apparent good health and vigor. At the lunch hour he sat down to relax and read his Bible. He opened to the twenty-first chapter of Revelation and read John's words, "I saw a new heaven and a new earth."

"Emily," he said to my grandmother, "it will be wonderful when we see with our eyes the world that we can now only see by faith. . . ."

My grandmother glanced up from clearing the table because she expected him to say more. But grandfather's head had slumped forward and he was, no doubt, gazing upon that world of which he had just been speaking—for he loved the Lord Jesus very deeply. Years before he had learned that what Jesus had told Nicodemus was true, that unless a man is born anew, "he cannot see the kingdom of God" (John 3:5).

And, indeed, Christ is much more than the true money master of the world. He is a friend to sinners—the only one able to save them. So, when a man bows his will to God's will and accepts His pardon, he receives the gift of eternal life which Christ desires to bestow on all men. And His kingdom comes within.